DAVE BARRY'S

MONEY
$ECRETS

Also by Dave Barry

DAVE BARRY'S

MONEY $ECRETS

LIKE:

Why Is There a Giant Eyeball on the Dollar?

Crown Publishers / New York

Complete text for permissions appears on page 230.

Copyright © 2006 by Dave Barry

All rights reserved.
Published in the United States by Crown Publishers, an imprint of the
Crown Publishing Group, a division of Random House, Inc., New York.

Crown is a trademark and the Crown colophon is a
registered trademark of Random House, Inc.

ISBN-13: 978-0-7394-7193-7
ISBN-10: 0-7394-7193-7

Printed in the United States of America

Design by Lenny Henderson

This book is dedicated to all the people of the world, on the theory that they will respond by thinking: "Wow! A book dedicated to me. I should buy a copy."

ACKNOWLEDGMENTS

I want to thank Alan Greenspan, Milton Friedman, and the entire faculty of Harvard Business School for not attempting in any way to interfere with the writing of this book. I also want to thank Donald Trump and Suze Orman just for being who they are.

CONTENTS

DAVE BARRY'S

MONEY
$ECRETS

INTRODUCTION

WHY YOU NEED THIS BOOK

PERHAPS YOU'RE A YOUNG PERSON just getting started in life. Or perhaps you're an older person thinking about retiring. Or perhaps you're a hostile space alien planning to wipe out humanity by putting tiny radioactive scorpions in the latte machines at Starbucks.

Well, no matter who you are, *you need this book.*

"Why?" you ask.

Because chances are that when it comes to your personal finances, you are, with all due respect, a complete moron. I do not mean that in a derogatory way. I mean it simply in the sense that, when it comes to handling money, you are a stupid idiot.

"But," you say, "what if I follow the accepted principles of sound money management?"

Great. Except that your so-called "accepted principles of sound money management" are worthless.

"But," you say, "what if *OUCH!*"

I apologize for slapping your face, but if you keep interrupting with your stupid questions, we're never going to get through this introduction.

As I was saying, your so-called "accepted principles of sound money management" are worthless. To help you understand why, let's consider the financial situations of two best friends, named "Bob" and "John."

In some ways, "Bob" and "John" are very much alike: They're the same age, make the same salary, and have the same number of dependents. They live in identical houses next door to each other. They both have quotation marks around their names.

But that is where the similarities end. "Bob" is very involved in managing his money: He reads every money-related article he can get his hands on, follows all the money-advice experts on radio and TV, and regularly attends investment seminars.

"John" does none of these things. He has never read a word about money management. He has no investment plan. "John" can't even balance his checking account!

And yet, oddly enough, "Bob" is the one in financial trouble. He lives paycheck to paycheck. He can't afford to send his kids to college. He drives an old clunker car and is forced to use cheap, generic toilet tissue that makes him feel as though he is performing intimate hygiene with roofing materials.

"John," meanwhile, drives a new Mercedes, sends his kids to Ivy League universities, and dines at fine restaurants serving shrimp the size of Mike Tyson's forearm.

How is this possible? What is "John"'s secret? Simple: He is stealing from "Bob." He dug a tunnel under "Bob"'s house and uses it to swipe "Bob"'s cash, food, electricity, cable TV, and small appliances. Sometimes, when "Bob" is at an investment seminar, "John" has sex with "Bob"'s wife, "Alice."

What is the moral of this story? Simple: When it comes to money, *you can't even trust your best friend.* You can't trust *anybody.* Everywhere you turn, people are trying to take advantage of you.

I'll give you an embarrassing example from my own personal experience. Like many computer users, I receive a tremendous amount of "spam" e-mail. Most of it is highly questionable, consisting of offers to sell me discount Viagra, enlarge my penis, refinance my mortgage, eliminate my debts, get me a "great deal" on life insurance, set me up in some "home business" that will allegedly give me a huge income for just a few hours' work, enroll me in a pyramid scheme or some other "foolproof" system to "get rich quick" with almost no effort, and on and on and on. It's ridiculous! I mean, why would I need to enlarge MY penis? The very idea is absurd! Ask anyone!

But some of the "get rich quick" proposals look pretty good. I got one in particular from a businessman in Nigeria, who wrote me a very businesslike e-mail stating that, in a nutshell, he wanted to send me $47 million.

I didn't totally follow his explanation—there were a *lot* of details—but the gist was that there was some kind of business screwup over there in Nigeria (you know how it is in business) and a bunch of businesspeople decided that, for business reasons, they needed to send somebody $47 million, and somehow my name came up.

It seemed almost "too good to be true." But as I say, the e-mail was very businesslike, so I replied that, sure, I would be willing to take the $47 million.

You probably know what happened next. After a few e-mail exchanges, the businessman informed me that some "minor technical problems" had cropped up—something about "Nigerian government red tape"—and that in order to "smooth things out" and send the money to me, he needed me to send *him* an "advance fee" of $5,000.

I was a little suspicious, and my friends warned me to be cautious, but $5,000 seemed like a small enough investment for a return of $47 million. So I sent a check.

No sooner had it cleared than my businessman "friend" sent me another e-mail, apologizing and saying that there were more problems, and he needed *another* $5,000.

At this point my friends were all telling me that I had become the victim of a classic "scam," and that I was crazy to send any more money. But I was so blinded by greed, so hooked on the idea of getting my hands on this huge fortune, that I went ahead and wrote a second $5,000 check.

Two days later, I received $47 million in cash. It came via UPS in 578 large cardboard boxes. I have cash all over my house. If I want a helicopter, I just grab a box and go buy one. My money worries are over forever! And why? *Because I did not trust my friends.* They're not even my friends anymore, now that I'm extremely rich. I hang out with new friends that I met at the helicopter store.

Of course I cannot guarantee that you will achieve the same level of financial success as I did. But I *can* promise you that, if you carefully follow the proven, time-tested money-management principles[1] detailed in this book, you will be the first person ever to do so. And surely that is worth *something*.

So let's get started! The first order of business is for you to take the following:

Quiz to Determine
Your Current Financial Health

What kind of financial shape are you in right now? This scientific quiz will show you. Be honest in your answers: If you lie, you'll only be lying to yourself! The place to lie is on your federal tax return.

---

[1] I'll think of some. Trust me!

What is your annual income?
1. More than $50,000.
2. Less than $50,000.
3. However much I get when I return these empties.

Not counting your mortgage, how much money do you currently owe?
1. Less than $10,000.
2. More than $10,000.
3. Men are threatening to cut off my thumbs.

How would you describe your portfolio?
1. Conservative, mainly bonds and blue-chip equities.
2. Aggressive, mainly options and speculative stocks.
3. My what?

When analyzing an investment, what do you consider to be the most important factor?
1. The amount of return.
2. The degree of risk.
3. The name of the jockey.

How do you plan to finance your retirement?
1. Savings.
2. Social Security.
3. Sale of kidneys.

Calculating Your Score

- If your answers are mostly ones and twos, you're in pretty good financial health.
- If your answers are mostly twos and threes, you definitely need to improve your money-management skills.

- If your answers are *all* threes, be advised that we're having a minor technical problem calculating your score because of Nigerian red tape. To smooth things out, we need you to send us an "advance fee" of $5,000, which you will get back many times over.

1

HOW MONEY WORKS

Or: Everybody Clap for Tinker Bell!

WHY IS MONEY VALUABLE? Why are people willing to work so hard for it, lie for it, cheat for it, go to prison for it, fight for it, kill for it, give up their children for it . . . *even marry Donald Trump for it?*

I mean, look at the dollar bill. What is it, really? It's a piece of paper! What's more, it's a piece of paper that appears to have been designed by a disturbed individual. On one side, you have a portrait of George Washington, who, granted, was the Father of Our Country and a great leader and everything, but who looks, in this particular picture . . .

. . . like a man having his prostate examined by Roto-Rooter. And then on the *other* side of the dollar you have:

What is *that* about? Why is there a picture of a pyramid, instead of a structure traditionally associated with the fundamental values of the United States of America, such as a Wal-Mart? And why is the pyramid being hovered over by an eyeball the size of a UPS truck?

Whatever the explanation, the design of the dollar would not seem to inspire confidence in its value. And yet if you drop a few dollars from an overpass onto a busy freeway at rush hour, people will run into traffic and literally risk their lives in an effort to grab them. Try it!

What does this tell us? It tells us that people are stupid. But it also tells us that money is more than just pieces of paper. But what makes it valuable? To answer that question, we need to consider:

The History of Money

In prehistoric times, there was no such thing as money. When people needed to buy something, they had to charge it. And then when the bills came, nobody could understand them, because there was also no such thing as reading. This led to a lot of misunderstandings and hitting with rocks.

The first form of money that we are aware of by looking it up on the Internet was animals. From the start there were problems with this type of money, particularly the smaller denominations, such as squirrels, which were always biting the payee and scampering away.

By 9000 B.C., the most commonly accepted form of animal money was cattle. When you bought something, you would give the other person a cow, and the other person would give your change in calves. This was better than squirrels, but still not an efficient system. The cash registers were disgusting.

By 3000 B.C., the Mesopotamians[2] had invented two concepts that revolutionized economic activity: (1) writing and (2) banking. This meant that, for the first time, it was possible for a Mesopotamian to walk into a bank and hand the teller a stone tablet stating:

GIVE ME ALL YOUR COWS AND NOBODY GETS HURT

These robbers were captured quickly, because they had to make their getaways at very slow speeds. Still, it was clear that a better medium of exchange was needed.

The ancient Chinese tried to solve the problem by using seashells as money. The advantage of this system was that seashells were small, durable, clean, and easy to carry. The drawback was that they were, in a word, seashells. This meant that anybody with access to the sea could get them. By the time the ancient Chinese had figured this out, much of their country was the legal property of gulls.

And so the quest continued for a better form of money. Various cultures experimented with a number of commodities, including tea, grains, leather, tobacco, and Pokémon cards. Then, finally, humanity hit upon a medium of exchange that had no disadvantages—a medium that was durable, portable, beautiful, and universally recognized to have lasting value. That medium, of course, was beer.

No, seriously, it was precious metals, especially gold and silver, which—in addition to being rare and beautiful—could be easily shaped into little disks that fit into vending machines.

Before long, many cultures were using some form of gold for

---

2. Official cheer: *WE don't! WE don't WE don't Meso ROUND!*

money. It came in a wide variety of shapes and designs, as we see in these photographs of ancient coins unearthed by archeologists:

SOURCE: The British Museum of Really Old Things

The problem was that gold is too heavy to be constantly lugged around. So, to make it easier for everybody, governments began to issue pieces of paper to represent gold. The deal was, whenever you wanted, you could redeem the paper for gold. The government was just *holding your gold for you.* But it was YOUR gold! You could get it anytime! That was the sacred promise that the government made to the people. That's why the people trusted paper money. And that's why, to this very day, if you—an ordinary citizen—go to Fort Knox and ask to exchange your U.S. dollars for gold, you will be used as a human chew toy by large federal dogs.

Because the government changed the deal. We don't have the gold standard anymore. Nobody does. Over the years, all the governments in the world, having discovered that gold is, like, *rare,* decided that it would be more convenient to back their money with something that is easier to come by, namely: nothing. So even though the U.S. government still allegedly holds tons of gold in "reserve," you can no longer exchange your dollars for it. You can't even *see* it, because visitors are not allowed. For all you know, Fort Knox is filled with Cheez Whiz.

Which brings us back to the original question: If our money

really is just pieces of paper, backed by nothing, why is it valuable? The answer is: *Because we all believe it's valuable.*

Really, that's pretty much it. Remember the part in *Peter Pan* where we clap to prove that we believe in fairies, and we save Tinker Bell? That's our monetary system! It's the Tinker Bell System! We see everybody *else* running around after these pieces of paper, and we figure, *Hey, these pieces of paper must be valuable.* That's why if you exchanged your house for, say, a pile of acorns, everybody would think you're insane; whereas if you exchange your house for a pile of dollars, everybody thinks you're rational, because you get . . . pieces of paper! The special kind, with the big hovering eyeball!

And you laughed at the ancient Chinese, with the seashells.

So what does all this mean? Does it mean that our monetary system is a giant house of cards that would collapse like, well, a giant house of cards if the public stopped believing in the pieces of paper? Could all of our "wealth"—our savings, our investments, our pension plans, etc.—suddenly become worthless, meaning that the only truly "wealthy" people would be the survivalist wing nuts who trade all their money for guns and beef jerky?

Yes. But that probably won't happen. Because, fortunately, the public prefers not to think about economics. Most people are unable to understand their own telephone bills, let alone the U.S. monetary system. And as long as we don't question the big eyeball, Tinker Bell is safe.

OK, now you know what money actually is. (Don't tell anybody!) The next question is: How come some people have so *much* money, while others have so little? Why does the money distribution seem so unfair? Why, for example, are professional athletes paid tens of millions of dollars a year for playing silly games with balls, while productive, hardworking people with infinitely more value to society, such as humor writers, must struggle to make barely half that? And above all, how can *you*, personally, get more money?

We'll address these questions in future chapters,[3] which will be chock-full of sure-fire, can't-miss, no-nonsense, common-sense, easy-to-apply, on-the-money hyphenated phrases. You'll be on your way to riches in no time! All you have to do is *really believe* in yourself! Come on, show that you really believe! Clap your hands!

Also, just in case, you should get some jerky.

Why Does the Back of the Dollar Have a Pyramid and a Giant Eyeball?

There is actually a simple explanation for these two seemingly odd symbols:

Back when the Founding Fathers were designing our currency, they were looking for an image for the new nation, an image that would symbolize the concept of something strong and massive being watched over by something all-seeing and wise. After much discussion, what they came up with—as you have probably guessed—was a picture of an owl standing on an elephant.

The Founding Fathers passed this idea along to the artist hired to do the engraving of the printing plates for the dollar, whose name was Phil. As it happened, the day he did the dollar, which was his birthday, Phil consumed what historians now believe was at least two quarts of whiskey, and for whatever reason—the only explanation he ever gave was "the squirrels made me"—he engraved a pyramid with a giant eyeball on top of it.

---

3. Although not necessarily in *this* book.

Unfortunately, the Founding Fathers, who were in a hurry to get the dollar printed so they could spend it, failed to notice this until it was too late. Fortunately, however, they did catch the error on the front of the dollar, where, instead of George Washington, Phil had engraved a fish playing tennis. Otherwise we might live in a very different nation today.

2

HOW THE U.S. ECONOMY WORKS

Adam Sandler Is Involved

THE ECONOMY IS A LARGE, complicated thing that is difficult for regular untrained people like you to understand. Fortunately, in college I took economics for the better part of an entire semester, during which I took time out from my busy schedule to attend several actual classes. So in this chapter I will explain how the economy works, with certain key words in boldface type to indicate that they are darker than the other words.

The largest single item in the economy is the **Gross National Product,** or **DNA** for short. This consists of everything that is produced by the **labor force** after the labor force finally gets to work and finds a parking space and has some **Starbucks.** At one time the Gross National Product consisted of both **goods** and **services,** but today pretty much all physical objects are manufactured in **Asia,** which means the U.S. workforce is engaged in the **service economy,** consisting of **83 million people in cubicles** furtively sending and receiving **personal e-mails.** Also there is a small remaining **agriculture sector,** consisting of maybe 15 people in **Nebraska** or someplace who grow **soybeans,** although nobody knows what they do with them.

The sum total of the Gross National Product is **several trillion dollars,** of which one third is sent to the **government** in the form of **taxes** for the express purpose of being **wasted.** Another third goes directly to **Bill Gates.** The remaining third is divided up into **wages** and **prices,** which go **up** and sometimes, in the case of wages, **down,** in response to the **law of supply and demand,** which states that if there are fewer than two outs with runners on first and second base . . . no, sorry, that's the **infield fly rule.** The law of supply and demand states that if you have too much of something that not enough people really want, such as **movies starring Adam Sandler,** the price is going to go down until it reaches $1.99 per DVD; whereas if there is an *under*supply of something, such as whatever toy every child in America including yours wants for Christmas, but the toy manufacturer makes only 25 units of this toy for the entire freaking **world,** you will pay however much it costs you to get it after trading punches with other parents at **Toys Backwards "R" Us.**

If all the prices in the nation go down at once, that is called **deflation,** and the way to correct it is to wake up from the **dream** you are having, because this never happens in real life. In real life, all the prices always go up, a condition that economists call **inflation,** or, for short, **normal.** If inflation gets to be too bad, **Congress** holds a **hearing** at which the nation's **leading economists,** using sophisticated **data collection** and **computerized modeling,** present a **detailed statistical analysis** of the economic situation, after which they light a **bonfire** and sacrifice a **live virgin congressional intern.**

The resulting aroma summons **Alan Greenspan**[4], who is the chairman of the **Federal Reserve Board,** a mysterious organization that controls the **economy** from its secret **Batcave-style** headquarters far beneath the surface of the **earth.**

When Greenspan emerges from the ground, he looks around at the economy to determine whether he can see his **shadow.** In this respect, he is similar to the professional groundhog **Punxsutawney Phil,** although as we see in the photographs below, there are distinct physical differences between the two:

    Punxsutawney Phil   **Alan Greenspan**

After he has looked around, Greenspan makes an **ambiguous remark,** and everybody tries to figure out what it means. This is not easy, because Greenspan is crafty in his choice of words. For example, two years ago, in a speech before the Economics Council of London, Greenspan said: "What has one foot on each side and one in the middle?" This remark sent shock waves throughout the world economy. Investors lost more than $14 trillion in the resulting stock market plunge, and several hundred corporations went bankrupt, with a resulting loss of millions of jobs. It

---

4. After I wrote this, I found out that Alan Greenspan is retiring, so feel free to disregard this chapter. For that matter, feel free to disregard this book.

wasn't until nearly a month later that economists figured out that the answer to Greenspan's question was: **a yardstick.** But by then the damage had been done.

Sometimes these misunderstandings aren't really Greenspan's fault. The stock market crash of 1987 resulted from an incident at a luncheon when he was simply trying to tell the waiter that he wanted ranch dressing instead of vinaigrette.

If the economy appears to be heading for real trouble, Greenspan will raise or lower the **prime rate.** This is a very important economic thing, but unfortunately I was unable to attend the specific classes in which it was discussed.

The United States also engages in **international trade** with other nations, wherein we buy things that they produce such as **cars, computers, televisions, clothing, furniture, steel, cell phones,** and **pretty much everything else,** and in return they buy things that we produce, such as **Starbucks franchises** and **movies starring Adam Sandler.** If they fail to buy enough things from us, we have a **trade deficit,** and if it gets really bad, we have to remind everybody that in addition to Adam Sandler we have a lot of **nuclear missiles.**

Whew! It has been a lot of work, explaining the entire U.S. economy, but now that I'm done, you know as much about how it works as the people who are actually running it. You probably think I'm kidding.

3

MANAGING YOUR
PERSONAL FINANCES

REMEMBER THE FABLE of the grasshopper and the ant? The industrious ant worked hard all summer long, harvesting pieces of food dropped on the sidewalk in front of a Taco Bell. But the lazy grasshopper spent the summer frolicking and downloading Internet porn.

When fall came, the ant was snug in his anthill with a wad of rancid salsa the size of a volleyball. But the grasshopper had nothing to eat. He went to the ant's nest and said, "I'm starving! Can I have some . . . *YUCK!* What's that *smell?*"

"That's my food supply!" said the ant, who was a generous ant, "and I will gladly share it with y . . ."

FWOOSH

At that moment they were both burned alive, because the ant had built his nest in a playground frequented by inquisitive young boys with access to lighter fluid.

What financial lesson does this fable teach us? It teaches us that, in selecting real estate, the three most important factors are: location, location, location. But this chapter is not about real estate. This chapter is about managing your personal finances.

Do you have a good "handle" on where your money goes? To find out, ask yourself if the following statements describe you:

- You'd *like* to save money for the future, but it seems there's never any left over after you pay your bills.
- You have several credit cards, and you can never quite get the balances down to zero.
- You make large purchases on impulse.
- When you buy things, you often receive pennies in change, and you put these in a jar or some other container. Over the years you have accumulated roughly 17,000 loose pennies. At one point, you actually bought penny wrappers, but you never put the pennies in them, and you no longer know where the wrappers are, and you have heard that the banks don't really want them anyway. You frankly have no idea why the government still MAKES pennies. All you know is that you are going to die with these fricking pennies in your possession.
- When you wake up in the morning, you have to pee.
- Twice a year, you change all your clocks by an hour, but you don't really know why.
- You occasionally bet on sporting events, and you secretly believe that, by doing certain things such as positioning your hands in a certain way, or not looking directly at the television set, you can affect the accuracy of a field goal kicker thousands of miles away.
- You have convinced yourself that your sexual fantasies are normal.
- Even the one involving the penguin.
- At weddings, when the organ plays "Here comes the bride," your brain immediately responds with: "Big, fat, and wide."
- When you watch *The Wizard of Oz*, it troubles you that Glinda,

the so-called "Good Witch of the North," is actually quite *nonhelpful* to Dorothy. Like, at the beginning, she's all vague about the power of the ruby slippers, as if she has *no idea* what they can do, and then at the end, when Dorothy has gone through living hell to kill the Wicked Witch of the West so she can go back to Kansas, Glinda shows up and—guess what!—she knows *exactly* how Dorothy can use the slippers to get home. When the Scarecrow asks Glinda how come she didn't just explain this to Dorothy in the first place, Glinda gives a lame explanation about how Dorothy wouldn't have believed her, when in fact from the start Dorothy *totally* believed *everything* Glinda told her, including this *lie* that the "Wizard of Oz" was great and powerful, when in fact he was a drunk with a smoke machine (as if Glinda wouldn't know *that*). So what is clearly happening here is that Glinda was just *using* Dorothy to kill the Wicked Witch of the West. What a bitch.

- Speaking of movies: When you're at a movie theater, and your movie is about to start, you *always* end up in the concession line that doesn't move because the people in front just *can't decide* what they want, as if they're up there trying to negotiate a Middle East peace settlement instead of choosing between popcorn and Milk Duds—FOR GOD'S SAKE WILL YOU MORONS JUST *MAKE UP YOUR MINDS??*
- Sometimes, when nobody is around, you scratch your private parts with a hairbrush.
- You do not keep a detailed household budget.

If any one of these statements caused you to think: "That's me, all right!" then your personal finances are in serious trouble. What can you do about it?

One important step, of course, is to purchase products carrying the brand of a popular financial guru such as Suze "Suze" Orman. If you don't know who Suze is, turn on your TV right now and tune it to any channel, including the Cartoon Network. There she'll be:

Suze always has a smile on her face—the radiant, confident smile of a person who will not hesitate to kill anybody who gets in her way. But she's also smiling because she has helped millions of people who have learned the secrets of wealth by purchasing her many bestselling books and audiotapes, including *Suze Orman's Financial Guidebook; The Road to Wealth: A Comprehensive Guide to Your Money; The Laws of Money, the Lessons of Life; You've Earned It, Don't Lose It; 9 Steps to Financial Freedom; The Courage to Be Rich; Here's Yet Another Suze Orman Book About Money; You Might Think That at Some Point Suze Orman Would Run Out of Ideas for Money Books, but You Would Be Wrong;* and *Buy This Money Book or Suze Orman Will Rip Out Your Throat with Her Large Carnivorous Teeth.*

The reason Suze has sold so many books is that she offers a clear, simple, common-sense message that resonates with everyday people: *You pathetic loser.*

As Suze explains, because of your loserhood, you're probably doing many stupid things with your money that you're not even aware of. For example, let's say that, every morning on the way to work, you stop at Starbucks and buy a latte for $3.95. It doesn't sound like much, does it? But suppose that, instead of spending that money on coffee, you set it aside each day. What would happen?

First of all, without the caffeine, you'd fall asleep in your cubicle at work and get fired. But look at the financial upside! At the end of just two working weeks, you'd have saved $3.95 per day for ten days, which works out to, let's see . . . carry the 6 . . . OK, it's nearly *forty dollars*. That's right: You would have saved enough money to invest in *a half keg of beer*—enough, if you manage it properly, to maintain a serious buzz for *an entire weekend*. THAT'S the kind of long-term financial thinking Suze and I are talking about.

But to achieve this kind of result, you need to develop, and stick to, a Personal Financial Plan. If you're like most people, you're always thinking of reasons why you haven't made a Personal Financial Plan, like "I don't have the time," or "I'm no good with numbers," or "I'm being held prisoner in a cave by a lunatic who believes he is taking orders from a bat."

Well, Mr. or Ms. Excuse-Maker, it's time you stopped whining and started taking charge of your financial situation. It's easy! You just need to follow these steps:

1. **Analyze your cash flow.** "Cash flow" is a term that accountants use to describe the flowing of cash. To analyze your cash flow, first sit down at your kitchen table, put your head in your hands, and think really hard about the following question: "Where the HELL does all my money go?"

When you have figured out the answer, you should make a pie chart to help you graphically visualize your cash flow. It should look something like this:

Where Your Money Goes

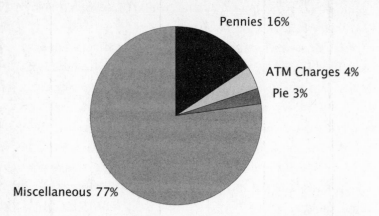

Pennies 16%

ATM Charges 4%

Pie 3%

Miscellaneous 77%

When we analyze this chart, we see that your biggest area of concern, cash-flow-wise, is your Miscellaneous. This is where you need to cut back, by not spending so much money on frivolous and unnecessary items. Your children, for example. Chances are that, like most kids today, they want you to buy them every new fad item that comes along, so they can be like their friends. Be firm with them! Tell them: "Just because your friends have food, clothing, and medical care, that doesn't mean YOU have to have those things." (We'll have more on reducing the high cost of children in our chapter on education, under "Steering Your Child Away from Harvard and Toward a Cheap, Crappy College.")

You can also save on your household expenses by using time-tested homeowner money-saving tips. For example: Do you use toilet paper? Of course you do! No shame in that. But when you've used up the roll, what do you do with the little cardboard tube? You throw it away, right? I bet that, over the years, you've thrown away hundreds of those little tubes. But if you save them in a box, at some point down the road you'll have collected enough so that you can put them to some kind of clever, money-saving household use. Although it beats the hell out of me what that use might be. I'm a financial expert, not Heloise.

Another way you can save money is to avoid using your credit cards. Oh, sure, it's easy to "whip out the plastic," but it's also a bad idea. Let's say you're at a convenience store, and you buy a can of Diet Coke costing a dollar, which you pay with your credit card. For openers, the people in line behind you—especially if I am one of them—will silently curse you, because now they all have to wait while the cashier gets authorization from Taiwan or Mars or wherever for your stupid one-dollar purchase.

But also, that purchase is going to be more expensive than you think. By the time you have completely eliminated all traces of it from your credit card statement, that "one-dollar" Diet Coke will have cost you—get ready—$386.52!

Does that seem like an absurdly high number? OK, let's analyze it. Assume that your credit card company charges you an annual percentage rate of 14.4 percent, and that you pay one half of your balance each month. Now do the math.

Ha ha! I am just kidding, which I will indicate here by inserting the international symbol for lighthearted jesting:

Suze and I are laughing because we know that there is no way in hell that you can do the math. I can't either! I just made up the $386.52. This, I believe, is also what the credit card companies do. I believe they put random, meaningless numbers on our statements, because they know that we, their clueless, math-impaired customers, will not challenge them. It would not surprise me to learn that the credit card companies have an industry-wide competition to see who can get a consumer to accept the most absurd credit card balance. Each year they announce the winner at a big awards banquet:

MASTER OF CEREMONIES: Our winner this year is Wanda Zuckmiller of Visa, who achieved what many experts in our industry said was impossible: She mailed out the first Visa statement ever with a balance of—and this is a direct quote— "one jillion dollars." Not only did the credit card holder, a Mrs. Shirley Hemplerigger of Plano, Texas, unquestioningly accept this amount—her exact words were "I have GOT to stop buying collectible wax fruit on eBay"—but Wanda also got Mrs. Hemplerigger to sign a statement agreeing to pay off her balance by sending Visa $50 a month for—and again I am quoting—"87 bazillion months."

(WILD APPLAUSE)

Does this mean you should cut up your credit cards and throw them away? No. It just means that you should use them wisely. Suppose, for example, that you see an item in a store that you really need, but you don't have enough cash on hand to buy it. This is the logical time to use a credit card. Wait until the store closes, then slide the card into the door crack and use it to jimmy open the lock.

Ha ha! Suze and I are just pulling your leg again. It's against the law to break into stores, and a credit card is the wrong tool for the job.[5]

Our point is that there are many simple and effective techniques that you can use to reduce your unnecessary spending, and just because we haven't been able to think of any in this chapter, that is no excuse for you not to employ them. Suze and I are sick of your excuses.

---

5. We recommend a debit card.

4

HOW THE CORPORATE
WORLD WORKS

The Critical Role of Office Furniture

THE BEST WAY TO UNDERSTAND the corporate world is to open up any newspaper to the business section and read a story at random. Chances are it will say something like this:

TROUBLED AIRLINE ANNOUNCES
GIGANTIC LOSSES

Troubled Unideltican Airways today announced third-quarter losses amounting to $7.1 billion. This comes on top of second-quarter losses of $6.6 billion and first-quarter losses of $6.8 billion, meaning that so far in this year alone, the troubled airline has lost more money than the gross national product of Central America.

"Sweet Lord Jesus, this is troubling," commented Unideltican's chief executive officer, E. Harmon Swackette III. "Every time I come back from a golf tournament, there's another billion gone! I've never seen anything like it, except at the last six companies I was CEO of.

"Clearly we need to find more ways to cut costs," continued Swackette, a former executive in the troubled Internet-poultry industry who currently makes $17.3 million per year, including performance bonuses. "We saved some money by laying off nonessential personnel such as the whaddycallem, copilots. And of course we no longer feed the passengers, who now, on our longer routes, get so hungry that they eat the in-flight magazines. But we need to look in other areas, such as those big loud things on the wing, the whaddycallits, engines. My people tell me those things use a LOT of costly fuel. I'm thinking maybe they don't all have to be turned on all the time."

Swackette said the troubled airline would also be looking for new sources of revenue. "For example," he said, "after takeoff, we could make an announcement like, 'Once we reach a comfortable cruising altitude of 35,000 feet, you will be free to move about the cabin, although this may be difficult for our non-Sherpa passengers, because Unideltican Airways no longer offers cabin pressurization in coach. So those of you who plan to breathe during the flight might want to rent an oxygen canister for $138.75 from one of the flight attendants now passing down the aisle. As always, exact change is greatly appreciated! We're also selling a selection of condiments to put on your magazine.'"

Swackette added that if the troubled airline's losses continue, he would have "no choice but to seriously consider jacking up executive bonuses."

These stories aren't always about the airline industry. Every day there's news about large companies in other industries that, to judge from their losses, are setting fire to bales of cash in the parking lot. These stories teach us three important facts:

Fact 1: Large corporations are *really* rich, so rich that they can piss away ridiculous amounts of money and still remain large.

Fact 2: These companies pay excellent salaries to top executives, who, to judge from Fact 1 . . .

Fact 3: . . . do not necessarily know any more about how to run a business than you, or, for that matter, a reasonably bright Labrador retriever.

Ask virtually any employee of virtually any large corporation about the competence of the people in charge, and you will be assured that they are complete morons whose apparent goal is to destroy the company. High-level-executive moronity is a universally observed phenomenon, although nobody really knows what causes it. The most plausible theory is executive office furniture. This theory holds that, in small quantities, there is nothing harmful about your quality hardwoods such as walnut, oak, mahogany, Formica, etc. But apparently when you have a very large mass of this type of wood—as you would find in the office of your typical high-level corporate executive, who, to indicate his executive stature, has a desk with the same surface area as Vermont—the wood emits some kind of invisible Stupid Rays that penetrate and ravage the brain of any human who remains too long within range, as depicted in the following scientific diagram:

How Executive Office Furniture Shrinks the Human Brain

SOURCE: The Mayo Clinic

Furniture Induced Brain Shrinkage (FIBS) is the only possible explanation for certain unbelievably bad decisions made by theoretically intelligent executives in charge of huge corporations with access to vast amounts of data:

(**The scene: The executive conference room of the Coca-Cola Corp., 1984. The CEO rises to speak.**)

CEO: Gentlemen, our primary product, Coca-Cola, is the number one soft drink in the world. The question is: What are we, as highly paid executives, going to do about this? Anybody have any suggestions?

(**There is a lengthy pause, while everybody thinks hard, staring at the table. Finally, a hand goes up.**)

CEO: Yes, Bob?
BOB: I have one.
CEO (*puzzled*): One what?

BOB: Suggestion.

CEO: Oh! Right! What is it?

BOB (*puzzled*): What is what?

CEO: What's your suggestion?

BOB: Oh! Right! I was thinking maybe we could change it.

(**DEEP FROWNS OF PUZZLEMENT ALL AROUND THE TABLE.**)

CEO: Change *what*, Bob?

BOB: Change the product.

(**EVEN DEEPER FROWNS AROUND THE TABLE.**)

BOB: Coca-Cola.

(**SMILES, NODS OF RECOGNITION AROUND THE TABLE.**)

CEO (*thoughtfully*): So, Bob, if I understand you correctly, you're saying that we should take Coca-Cola—which is not only the most successful soft drink in history, but also the single most successful product of *any kind* in history; a product whose formula has remained the same for nearly 100 years; a product whose consumers are fiercely loyal—and you're saying we should *change* it?

BOB: Yes.

CEO: I like it!

(**NODS AROUND THE TABLE; MURMURS OF "I LIKE IT, TOO!" AND "ME TOO!" AND "WHAT ARE WE TALKING ABOUT, AGAIN?" AND "I WET MYSELF!"**)

CEO: Then it's settled! We'll change the formula! I'll call Research and Development!

(PAUSE)

CEO: Does anybody remember how to operate the phone?

Another example of a major corporation doing something that appeared to be clinically insane was the decision by General Motors—which must have an *enormous* executive conference table—to manufacture the Pontiac Aztek, a car so ugly that it routinely causes following motorists to go blind. I mean, OK, imagine you're a high-ranking GM executive, and the New Car Design Group comes to you with a proposal for a new car, and they show you *this* hideous image:

No! Sorry! Wrong image! They show you this:

Now, if your IQ is a positive number, you're going to look at this image, and you're going to have some questions. Such as:

- Who, exactly, is the target market for this vehicle? Does research show that there are a lot of potential car buyers out there saying, "I want a squat little car with a *really* big ass"?
- What are we going to call this vehicle? The ButtMobile? The HunchCar of Notre Dame?

But apparently no GM executives asked these questions. Instead, they chose to spend millions and millions of corporate dollars and actually *make* this car, which they called the "Aztek," which isn't even *spelled* right,[6] and if that isn't scientific proof that executive furniture destroys brain cells, I don't know what the hell is.

Or take my business, the newspaper business. I know many high-level newspaper executives, and individually they are all smart and wonderful people, especially the ones who have, for whatever reason, given me money. But when they get together to decide things, newspaper executives display the intelligence of soybeans.

Why do I say this? Consider:

For decades now, newspaper readership has been steadily going down. A major reason is that young people don't read newspapers. Young people either don't care about news, or prefer to get their news from alternative sources, such as the Internet, TV, cell phones, cereal boxes, skywriting, and other people's tattoos. But whatever the cause, these young people *do not read newspapers*.

As I say, the readership decline has been going on for decades. And over those decades, newspaper executives have tried many, many times to solve the problem. Unfortunately—and this is

---

6. The correct spelling is "Asstek."

what convinces me that exposure to office furniture must be involved—they *always come up with exactly the same solution, at newspaper after newspaper, despite the fact that it has never once, not a single time, actually worked.*

The solution they always come up with—after hiring consultants, doing extensive surveys, and holding many meetings—is *to appeal to younger people.* They always try to do this via a two-pronged approach:

- **Prong One:** Do fewer stories about heavy boring topics such as the world, and more stories about topics that, in the view of middle-aged newspaper executives, are of interest to young people who do not read newspapers. These youth-oriented topics include extreme sports, video games, hip-hop music, skateboarding, celebrities, tattoos, celebrity tattoos, and extreme-skateboarding hip-hop video-game celebrities with tattoos.
- **Prong Two:** Give the paper a jazzier, more youthful look by publishing more graphics, more bold colors, and more pictures of interest to young people who would not pick up a newspaper if their lives depended on it. Make stories shorter, so that they do not contain so many pesky words. Make paragraphs shorter. Make sentences shorter. Use shorter words. Like this. If you *must* write about the world, write about countries with short names, such as Chad.

This two-pronged strategy always produces two results, both entirely predictable:

- **Result One:** Older people, the ones who actually read the newspaper, notice that their newspaper is starting to look and read like a cross between *The National Enquirer* and a comic book, and that it contains an inordinate number of stories about topics they have no interest in, such as hip-hop video skateboarding in Chad. Some of these older readers become disgusted and cancel their subscriptions.

•**Result Two:** Younger people pay no attention whatsoever, because, as we have noted, they do not read newspapers.

So, with some older readers canceling their subscriptions, and no young people signing up, the newspaper's readership, instead of going up, declines still more. This causes great consternation among newspaper executives, who hire more consultants, conduct more surveys, and, above all, hold many lengthy "brainstorming" sessions around large hardwood conference tables.

It is there that the newspaper executives, their brains shriveled to the size of quarks by Furniture Induced Brain Shrinkage, come up with what they sincerely believe to be a radical new plan for saving the newspaper: They'll appeal to younger readers! Do more stories on youthful topics! Redesign the paper so it has more graphics, shorter stories! Rub mayonnaise in their hair and sing "I Feel Pretty!"

Actually, I made that last one up, although it would probably do less harm to the newspaper industry than the other "fixes." Anyway, the newspaper executives barge mindlessly ahead with yet *another* Youth-Oriented Makeover. Like the seventeen previous Youth-Oriented Makeovers, it's a disaster, leaving the executives no choice but to hire more consultants, conduct more surveys, and once again gather 'round the old conference table, where they come up with a *radical new plan.* . . .

OK, you get the point (unless you're sitting next to office furniture, in which case you're thinking, "I don't get it! What's the point??"). And I don't mean to pick on the newspaper industry; it just happens to be the one I'm most familiar with. I'm sure you can cite plenty of examples of high-level corporate stupidity in your own industry. Virtually *all* modern businesses are run this way, which is why the primary activity of your modern corporation—far more important than actually making anything—is buying other corporations.

Here's how it works: Your typical corporation, as we have established, is run by a group of morons sitting around a conference table and making bad decisions. Eventually these decisions cause the corporation to suffer declining profits, or even outright losses. So the executives, instead of reaching the obvious conclusion—namely, that they are incompetent—conclude that *there must be something wrong with their entire industry.*

So they decide to buy a corporation in some *other* industry, generally one they know absolutely nothing about. Like, if their company makes brassieres, they might decide they want to own a chain of plumbing-supply stores. Or maybe even—why not?—an auto manufacturer. ("Let's make an offer on General Motors! I really love that Pontiac Aztek!")

So Company A buys Company B, only to discover that Company B, which of course is also run by functional morons, is not doing so hot either. So the combined managements of both companies gather together—they need a *really* big conference table for this—and decide that what they need to do, as executives making huge salaries, is fire some workers.

This strikes everybody at the conference table as a fine idea, because (a) workers cost money, and (b) none of them are sitting at the conference table. So they fire some workers and outsource their jobs to Asia. They keep doing this until eventually all the actual work is being done by people in some Third World village who are so happy not to be shoveling yak dung that they will work for an entire month in exchange for a roll of Certs.

Am I exaggerating? Of course I am. Many overseas workers receive only *half* a roll of Certs. But my essential point is true: If you want to make money in a modern corporation, you do *not* want to be a worker. You do not want to know *anything* useful or practical, such as how to make an actual brassiere. You want to be an *executive,* so you can sit around the conference table and make important, high-level, far-reaching strategic decisions with the other morons. In the next chapter, we'll talk about how you can achieve that goal.

5

HOW TO GET A JOB

The Amazing Power of Oral Sex

A S WE LEARNED IN THE LAST CHAPTER, your goal is to get a high-paying executive job in a big corporation. Unfortunately, this is not easy: For every good job opening you find, chances are there will be hundreds—even thousands—of people competing against you for it. There is simply no practical way you can kill them all.

But that is no reason to give up hope. Oh, sure, you and I both know, deep down inside, that the other job candidates are smarter and more competent than you. But competence and intelligence aren't everything. Look at the past ten or eleven presidents of the United States.

No, you *can* get the job, if you take certain steps. Step one is to:

1. Research Your Prospective Employer
When you apply for a job at a corporation, it's good to have some idea of what the corporation does. Sometimes you can tell by the corporation's name. For example, General Foods makes foods,

General Motors makes motors, General Mills makes mills, General Electric makes electricity, General Dynamics makes dynamics, and so on.

Note: If the corporation has a mutant name like "Amerisource" or "Accenture," chances are nobody knows what it does, including the people who work there.

There are other important things you should find out about a corporation you are thinking of working for, such as:

- Where, exactly, will you, as an executive, park?
- Will you get to use the corporation's skybox seats? For which games?
- What about the play-offs?
- Will you have Internet access? This is *very* important: You'll be spending a lot of time at work, and you will need something to do.
- When you call in sick because you need to do something else that day, can you just *say* you're sick, or do you have to really *sound* sick and provide explicit details of your pretend illness, such as, "I have never seen diarrhea spurt that far."
- How is the corporate cafeteria? Does it have a variety of entrées and a well-maintained salad bar, with the ingredients carefully separated? Or are there always some rogue chickpeas in the low-fat ranch dressing?
- What about eating out? Is the corporation located near decent restaurants? Or is it in some rural hellhole where the only off-site cuisine option is a Big Boy?
- Are there chickpeas in the Big Boy's low-fat ranch?
- What the hell *are* chickpeas, anyway?

Once you have gathered this information, it's time to move on to step two of the job-getting process:

2. Prepare Your Resume

Your resume (rhymes with "legume") is a list of qualifications that you sincerely want your prospective employer to believe you have. Remember that the people who look at your resume will also look at thousands of others, so if you want yours to stand out, it must be brief; it must be compelling; and it must contain a photograph of Angelina Jolie naked. So in preparing your resume, you should follow this format:

STANDARD BUSINESS RESUME FORMAT

Your Name
You can usually obtain this from your driver's license.

Your Nickname
This should be something that has a positive, businesslike ring to it, such as "The Deal Closer" or "The Profit Maker." It's important that you establish a good nickname *before* you start working at the corporation, to prevent your co-workers from giving you a bad one, such as "The Diarrhea Shooter."

Photograph of Angelina Jolie Naked
If you don't already have one, ask any teenage male.

Job Objective
This should be a clear description of your career goal, such as:

"To obtain a high-paying executive job with a reserved parking spot in, or at least near, the building."

Qualifications

This is the heart of the modern business resume. This is where we separate the sheep from the chaff. Because it is here, in the qualifications section, where you prove to a prospective employer that you possess the skill and knowledge necessary to string meaningless hyphenated buzzwords together into a sentence fragment lacking a grammatical subject.

> **Wrong:** *"I am a hard worker who gets along well with others."*
>
> **Right:** *"Results-oriented multitasking hands-on team-building problem-solving take-charge self-starter with enterprise-wide cross-functional productivity-enhancement management-specific capabilities including all phases of conceptualization, implementation, integration, augmentation, allocation, irrigation, fermentation, lactation, plantation, and antidisestablishmentarianism served over field greens with a balsamic vinaigrette."*

Don't worry if your qualifications sentence fragment does not make a ton of sense; after the first dozen or so buzzwords, your readers, satisfied that you are fluent in corporate bullshit, will bail out of this section and resume taking ganders at Angelina Jolie.

Note: If you think the corporation where you're trying to get a job does some kind of technical thing, your qualifications should include a statement of your technical qualifications:

> **Wrong:** *I can answer the telephone and operate a stapler.*
>
> **Right:** *Highly proficient in all phases of WURP and FREEMIS*

hierarchical algorithm cosine protocols, including Version 3.872 of GRIMPL.

Again, you need not worry about whether your technical statement actually means anything. The people reading your resume would never admit that they have no idea what WURP and FREEMIS are; they will simply assume that these are important technical things they should know about, and they will start referring to them in their own reports and memos.

Education

Your goal here is to establish your academic credentials. Be sure to word this very carefully, because you need to make a good impression.

> **Wrong:** *Attended Wayne P. Leeperman College of Refrigeration Arts and Sciences*
> **Right:** *Masters of Doctorate Degree in Business Exploitation, Harvard or Yale University*

There is a slight risk that somebody might start to become suspicious about your academic credentials, so this is a good point in your resume to include, as a distraction:

A Second Photograph of Angelina Jolie Naked

When you have completed your resume, send it to every employee at your target corporation above the rank of restroom attendant, along with a brief cover letter stating, in a businesslike and professional manner, that you are sincerely interested in obtaining a job and are willing to provide high-quality oral gratification to whoever will give you one.

Of course, I am jesting.[7] You just keep sending out your resume, and eventually, if you are persistent, you will receive a call from a top corporate executive—a person in a position to give you the job of your dreams—telling you that he or she will call the police if you don't stop sending your resume.

But don't let that stop you! Keep at it, and eventually some executive will want to talk to you, if only to find out if you have any more naked photos of Angelina Jolie. This means it's time for step three:

3. Prepare for Your Job Interview

Up to this point, you're just a name on a piece of paper. The interview is your chance to show your prospective employers that you are a real person, with real armpits gushing rivers of real sweat.

You have good reason to be nervous: The impression you make in your interview is absolutely crucial. You must appear confident without being cocky, relaxed without being indifferent, and tall without being short.

Your appearance is extremely important. Avoid common fashion "no-nos" such as showing up for an interview with twigs in your hair or a large albino python around your neck. Cover any visible tattoos with bandages or spray paint. Above all, make sure you are "dressed for success"—which means your clothing must look serious and professional.

---

7. Not really.

Dressing for Success in the Job Interview

Wrong   **Right**   **Wrong**   **Right**

SOURCE: Calvin Klein

But your appearance alone will not get you the job. You must show your interviewers that you will be a "good fit" in the culture of the specific corporation. Look for subtle ways to let your interviewers know that you have things in common with them, such as: "Nice to meet you! I, too, am a white person!" (Note: Depending on the interviewers, you should substitute "African-American," "Hispanic," "Native American," "person of some kind of Asiatic extraction," or "carbon-based life-form.")

It's also very important to demonstrate that you have a good sense of humor, as we see by the following verbatim transcript of an actual interview with a top New York investment banking firm:

INTERVIEWER: I see by your resume that you are proficient in both WURP and FREEMIS. Can you tell us about that?
YOU: Certainly. But first . . . ROO ROO!
INTERVIEWER: Ha ha! I love that joke! You are hired right on the spot.[8]

---

8. Another proven job-getter is the "Aristocrats" joke.

Be alert during the interview for "trap questions." These are questions that an interviewer asks to trick you into saying something negative about yourself.

Examples of "Trap Questions"

WHY DID YOU LEAVE YOUR LAST JOB?

Good Answer: I felt that I had accomplished all I could and was looking for a more challenging environment where I could make an effective contribution.

Bad Answer: The arson investigation was getting too close.

HOW DO YOU RESPOND TO CRITICISM FROM SUPERIORS?

Good Answer: I view it as a chance to improve myself by learning from those with more wisdom and experience.

Bad Answer: If they're so superior, how come they can't figure out who killed their dog?

WHAT WOULD YOU SAY IS YOUR BIGGEST WEAKNESS?

Good Answer: Sometimes I get so involved in my job that I tend to neglect my personal life.

Bad Answer: Heroin.

DESCRIBE A JOB-RELATED SITUATION THAT, IN RETROSPECT, YOU WISH YOU HAD HANDLED DIFFERENTLY.

Good Answer: Late one Friday night, in an effort to make sure I had reviewed every possible detail on a project that was important to my superiors, I fell asleep at my desk, which was unprofessional. I should have simply taken the project home and worked on it over the weekend.

Bad Answer: There was really no need to shoot that second bank guard.

Make sure to get the names of all the people you talk to, so that after your interview you can keep yourself fresh in their minds by writing them follow-up letters, phoning them, e-mailing them, and visiting them at home on weekends to remark on what a nice dog they have. Don't give up! Remember: In any large organization, the person who gets ahead is not necessarily the person who works the hardest or does the best job; it's the person who consistently displays the perseverance, assertiveness, and aggressiveness of the true leader.[9] You *can* be that leader.

---

9. In the sense of "asshole."

6

ETHICAL GUIDELINES
FOR CORPORATE CEOS

Beware the Penis That Squirts Vodka

WHEN YOU'RE THE CEO of a major corporation, you get a lot of perks—a huge salary, generous stock options, a big office, a corporate jet ready to whisk you to exclusive golf resorts, and a staff of lackeys to take your shirts to the laundry, wash your luxury car, clip your nasal hairs, and do all the other things that you, as a busy CEO, do not have time to do.

But with these benefits come the responsibilities of being a leader. Which *specific* exclusive golf resort should the corporate jet whisk you to? Do you want starch in your shirts? How *much* starch? Only you, as CEO, can make these decisions.

Also from time to time you might have to become involved in the running of the corporation per se. You must be very cautious here, because in recent years the authorities have become quite picky about enforcing rules that prohibit corporate executives from lying and stealing vast quantities of money. In a few cases, corporate executives have actually been convicted and sent to federal prisons, some of which have only the most rudimentary tennis courts.

You don't want anything that horrible to happen to you. So, if you become CEO, make sure you follow these ethical guidelines:

GUIDELINE NUMBER ONE: Keep your salary within reasonable limits.

More and more, the salaries of corporate CEOs are perceived, rightly or wrongly, as being out of line with the salaries of the, whaddyacallem, workers. So you want to make sure that, as CEO, your salary falls within reasonable limits. What do I mean by "within reasonable limits"? I mean "roughly 3,000 times as much as you pay a janitor."

If you don't know how much a janitor makes at your corporation, go to an employee bathroom and ask one. (If you don't know where the employee bathrooms are, ask one of your staff people.) Let's say the janitor tells you he makes $11,500 a year. Now, using a calculator (if you don't know how to operate a calculator, ask one of your staff people), simply multiply 11,500 times 3,000 to obtain your target salary, which in this case would be $34,500,000, or, rounding upward for bookkeeping convenience, $40 million.

Of course you may find that this is not enough. You may have a financial emergency, such as you're playing golf at an exclusive resort with another CEO and you find out that he makes *more* than $40 million a year. In this case, you have no choice but to increase your salary. But in order to do that and still remain within the ethical guidelines, you will need to increase the average salary of your janitors by one 3,000th of the amount of the raise you need (ask one of your staff people to figure out the exact numbers). Be advised that raising all these salaries might hurt your corporation's "bottom line." If so, you may have to compensate by firing some janitors. That won't be an easy decision to make, but that's why you, as CEO, make the big bucks.

> *GUIDELINE NUMBER TWO: If you use your corporation's money to pay for half of a lavish $2 million birthday party for your wife on the island of Sardinia, featuring, among many other lavish things, an ice statue of Michelangelo's David with vodka squirting out of its penis, for God's sake do not make a video of it.*

This was the mistake made by Dennis Kozlowski, who threw just such a party when he was CEO of Tyco. According to the Securities and Exchange Commission, Dennis also allegedly used company money to buy a shower curtain that cost $6,000 and a dog-shaped designer umbrella stand that cost $15,000. Dennis wound up getting into trouble, and a jury was shown a videotape of the party he threw for his wife. The defense claimed that the party was a legitimate business expense, which I am sure it was, based on this image from the video:

I mean, if those people are not conducting legitimate business, I would like to know exactly what the hell they *are* doing.

Unfortunately, if you wind up going to trial, you will be judged by a jury of ordinary lowlife non-CEO people who do not understand sophisticated business matters and, in many cases, have never spent so much as $1,000 for an umbrella stand. Yes, it is unfair. But that is the price we pay for living in a democracy.

> **GUIDELINE NUMBER THREE:** *Whatever else you do as Chief Executive Officer of the corporation, do not—repeat, do NOT—allow yourself to come into the possession of any information regarding specifically how the corporation works.*

This is very, very important. Because if the authorities decide that your corporation is doing bad things, they are going to try to hold somebody responsible, and often—unfair as it seems—they go after the person running the corporation. A chilling example is the case of Bernard "Bernie" Ebbers, who was CEO of WorldCom, a large corporation that got into a legal kerfuffle over some accounting hanky-panky involving, give or take, $11 billion. When Bernie went to trial, his defense, basically, was that he did not know what was going on inside the corporation. Oh, sure, he was the CEO and everything, and he was being paid many millions of dollars plus stock options, but as far as what WorldCom was actually *doing,* accounting-wise, Bernie was not in the loop. The defense did not come right out and use the phrase "total moron," but that was the gist of it.

Unfortunately for Bernie, the jury did not buy this defense. The jury apparently believed that somehow, in the course of being in charge of WorldCom, Bernie must have picked up some whiff of what was going on there. This is why it is so vitally important that, as CEO, you never, ever allow yourself to learn any details about your corporation. If you go to a meeting, and some corporate executives start talking about corporate business, put your hands over your ears and go, "LA LA LA LA, I CAN'T HEAR YOU!"[10]

---

10. This is also a good policy if you are president of the United States.

7

PROVIDING FOR MEDICAL CARE

You'll Need Some Leeches

I F YOU'RE LIKE MOST AMERICANS, your biggest single fear is that you'll become injured or seriously ill and have to be admitted to a hospital, where a psychopath posing as a nurse will sneak into your room one night, inject you with a paralyzing drug, and, while you're still fully conscious, remove both your eyeballs with a shrimp fork.[11] But coming in a close second is the fear of being unable to pay the medical bills.

Yes, medical care has become hideously expensive in this country. Go to any American hospital today to have even minor surgery such as removal of your tonsils, and you're looking at a minimum cost of $13,000. And that's just for *parking*.[12] The actual procedure will cost you way more.

Why is medical care so expensive? There is no one simple answer to this question, by which I mean: lawyers.

I'm not talking about *all* lawyers, of course. There are plenty

11. **Or maybe that's just me.**
12. **Rim shot.**

of good ones, such as . . . OK, Abraham Lincoln was a lawyer, right? He was pretty good. Also Raymond Burr. But the rest of them are scum.

This is especially true of the lawyers who make daytime-television commercials like this:

> (WE SEE A LAWYER, WEARING A SUIT AND TIE,
> LEANING AGAINST A DESK IN AN OFFICE.
> BEHIND HIM IS A SHELF FILLED WITH BOOKS.)

LAWYER: I'm Bernard Tortmonger of Tortmonger Legal Associates Legally Practicing Law. Are you in pain? Of *course* you are. Why else would you be watching daytime television? You're in pain, and that means somebody is responsible, and that means you need to SUE THEIR ASS.

("1-800-SUE-THEIR-ASS" IS SUPERIMPOSED ON THE SCREEN.)

LAWYER: Every day, we at Tortmonger Associates help people just like you get the money they have coming to them.

(WE SEE A VIDEO CLIP OF A MAN WEARING A NECK BRACE.)

MAN: I had no idea I had money coming to me. I was actually trying to call a phone-sex number and by mistake dialed Tortmonger Associates. They explained to me that I was in pain and helped me file a lawsuit. I won $600,000! Of course the Tortmonger Associates fee, plus standard legal expenses such as stapling, came to a total of $598,500. But I did get to keep this neck brace. Thanks, Tortmonger Associates!

LAWYER: You, too, have money coming, and Tortmonger Associates will fight to get it for you. We will kill for you if necessary, using our extensive knowledge of the law.

(HE GESTURES TO THE BOOKS BEHIND HIM, WHICH ARE ACTUALLY A COMPLETE SET OF THE 1953 ENCYCLOPAEDIA BRITANNICA.)

LAWYER: Although legal ethics prohibit me from making any promises about the outcome of your particular case, you will definitely win a huge amount of money. So call 1-800-SUE-THEIR-ASS now and let the experts at Tortmonger Associates help you decide exactly how much pain you are in. Remember: If you don't call, giant bats will suck out your blood. This must be true because it's on TV. Thank you.

Of course, the actual lawyer ads shown on television are not as subtle as this, but you get the idea. These ads are on all the time, the result being that Americans today are quick to sue their doctors for pretty much every bad medical thing that happens to them, including having to read an outdated issue of *Redbook* in the waiting room.

This has caused doctors to practice "defensive medicine," which means that to avoid getting sued, they often prescribe tests and procedures that are not clearly called for:

DOCTOR: OK, I want this patient to have an X-ray, sonogram, electrocardiogram, CAT scan, complete blood workup, lung biopsy, endoscopy, bronchoscopy, and extreme Roto-Rooter colonoscopy.

NURSE: He's not a patient. He's here to fix the phones.

DOCTOR: Then we'll also do a spinal tap.

So even a routine doctor visit can become very expensive. This is why you need medical insurance. The way it works is, every month, you or your employer sends money to an insurance company. Then, when you need expensive medical treatment, you notify the insurance company, which in turn notifies you that your treatment is not covered, or is only partially covered, as we see on this chart:

Your Health Insurance Benefits

Medical Condition	What Is *Not* Covered	What *Is* Covered
Arterial bleeding	Surgery, clamps, sutures, bandages, antibiotics	Mop
Sucking chest wound	Anesthesia, surgery	Cork
Cancer	Chemotherapy, radiation, surgery	Casket wreath[13]
Diabetes	Insulin	Leeches[14]
Hatchet embedded in skull	Removal of hatchet, treatment of wound	Larger hat
Eyes gouged out in hospital by psychopath posing as nurse	Prosthetic eyeballs, therapy	Six-pack

Source: The American Association of Big Insurance Companies That Did Not Get into the Insurance Business to Piss Money Away on the Likes of *You*

The bottom line is that, if you get injured or sick, you are financially screwed. So your wisest strategy is to stay healthy. Here are some ways you can do this:

---

13. **Up to $30.**
14. **Maximum of two.**

1. Don't smoke. Smoking is the nation's number one cause of cancer, emphysema, heart disease, death, ugly-ass teeth, and generally smelling like a fire at a condom factory. Also, many smokers—as a result of having to leave their smoke-free office buildings to go outside in the dead of winter and suck on cigarettes while snowdrifts pile up against their legs—are eaten by wolves.

And cigarettes are not just unhealthy: They're also absurdly expensive. As I write these words,[15] the average price of a single pack of twenty cigarettes is nearly *three dollars,* broken down as follows:

The Cost of a Pack of Cigarettes: Where the Money Goes

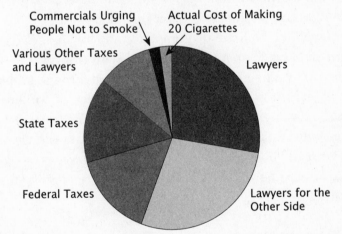

So smoking is an unbelievably stupid, expensive, evil, deadly addiction that benefits lawyers.[16] Why, then, do people do it? Many young people start smoking because they think it is "cool."

---

15. 9:33 a.m. Mountain Time.
16. I realize that this book has been pretty hard on lawyers. Be advised that the legal community will offer a thorough rebuttal in Chapter 27, titled "There Is No Chapter 27."

But it is not cool. It only *looks* cool. At least I believed it did when I smoked my first cigarette—a Kent, with the Micronite filter[17]— back when I was a fifteen-year-old assistant counselor at Camp Sharparoon.[18] My theory was that the Kent would cause female staff members to desire me in a carnal manner. But this is not what happened. What happened was I spent the evening on my hands and knees puking on the softball field. This is not something that women find attractive in a man. You rarely hear a woman say: "I'm looking for the kind of guy who is ralphing up a mess of lasagna on third base." But being a young, idealistic, determined moron, I continued working at smoking until I could do it without throwing up, which is the epitome of smoking pleasure. ("This is enjoyable! It's not making me vomit!")

Eventually, I realized that smoking was an insanely stupid activity, and I made up my mind to quit. Many smokers will try to tell you that quitting is hard, but I found that, through willpower and determination, I was able to quit "cold turkey," without any trouble, in just over a decade and a half. So take it from a former nicotine addict: If you're not a smoker, don't start. And if you are a smoker, can I bum a cigarette?

No, seriously, if you are a smoker, and you're applying for life insurance, lie.

2. Don't drink too much. Alcohol, like tobacco, is the nation's leading cause of death. It turns your liver into jerky and impairs your judgment. What do I mean by "impaired judgment?" OK,

---

17. Amazing but True Fact: At one time, Micronite filters were made out of asbestos.

18. Actual cheer: "Wanicko! Wanacko! Wanick Wanack Wano! Maroon! Maroon! Sharparoon!"

let's say you're sitting in a bar watching an NFL game, and a guy next to you makes some observation that you do not agree with— say, that the Green Bay Packers defensive backfield sucks. If you have *not* been drinking, chances are you will simply let the matter drop. Whereas, if you *have* been drinking, you will feel compelled to ask the guy exactly what kind of complete fricking moron he is, despite the fact that (1) the guy was addressing his observation to somebody else; (2) the guy is the size of a Federal Express truck; and (3) no member of the Green Bay Packers defensive backfield would ever, under any circumstances, stick up for *you*. These facts begin to penetrate your brain only later, as the Emergency Room doctor is explaining what foods you will be able to eat through the tube in your neck. That's what I mean by "impaired judgment."

Here are some other signs that you might be drinking too much:

- You find that you need a drink to settle your nerves when you are confronted with unexpected or upsetting occurrences, such as dawn.
- You sometimes make statements such as: "I bet you can't shoot this beer can off my head."
- You frequently engage in promiscuous sexual behavior, not always with members of your own species.
- You nod off at inappropriate times, such as at work, or while driving a motorcycle.
- You sometimes wake up on unfamiliar continents.
- You often see yourself featured on the TV show *Cops*, usually handcuffed facedown in front of a mobile home.
- You find that you spend a lot more time than other people searching for your pants.
- A recurring theme in your home decor is dried vomit.

If you notice five or more of these warning signs in your own life, you need to eliminate alcohol consumption altogether, or at least limit it only to certain very specific times, such as when you're awake.

3. Eat a healthy diet. Along with tobacco and alcohol, the number one cause of death in America is food. Americans eat way too much of it and have become a nation of enormous waddling giant-butted slugs. This is not their fault. It is the fault of the food industry, which deliberately makes food and foodlike products that Americans like to eat large amounts of.

A good example is Cheez-Its, which are chemically enhanced snack crackers the color of a radioactive traffic cone. Every time I go to my local supermarket, I am forced to walk directly past a flagrant, semipornographic Cheez-Its display, which apparently features a hidden motion-activated snack-flinging catapult, because somehow, without any conscious action on my part, I always end up with a large box of Cheez-Its in my shopping cart. This leaves me with no choice, as a husband and father desiring to protect his family from the threat of non-nutritious foods, but to eat the entire box[19] myself during the three-mile drive home from the supermarket. This is clearly bad for me, and I only hope that I am able to become part of a massive class-action lawsuit against Keebler before I become too large to fit into my car.

But suing the food industry, important as it is, may not be enough. We also need to accept some limited responsibility for what we insert into our personal mouths and swallow. Nutrition experts recommend that we eat a Healthy Balanced Diet based

---

19. That's right: Sometimes, in addition to the Cheez-Its, I eat the *actual box.*

on scientific principles, which sounds like a fine idea, except that these principles are apparently based on the nutritional needs of mutant rabbits. I say this because these diets always look like this:

HEALTHY DAILY DIET

- 27 servings raw fruit with those annoying little stickers still attached
- 153 servings raw green leafy vegetables such as kale
- .0063 kilogram nonendangered free-range fish, boiled
- 3 servings tree bark
- 43 servings uncooked dirt or gravel
- One live insect
- 126 gallons low-fat water

There are serious practical problems with these diets. Number one is, nobody knows what "kale" is. Number two is, no normal human with a job has either the time or the mathematical ability to prepare and keep track of all these "servings." Normal humans spend most of their days in a real-world work environment, where approximately 70 percent of their daily food intake is supplied by vending machines, and the closest available thing to a green leafy vegetable is mesquite-flavored potato chips.[20]

So the bottom line is, if you want to eat a Healthy Balanced Diet, you are going to have to develop the self-discipline to quit the junk-food habit and make the time to eat only sensible,

---

20. Now with Micronite filters!

healthy meals prepared in advance at home. Like you would *ever* do that. This leaves you with no choice but to SUE THEIR ASS!

4. Don't have sex. Sex, along with virtually every other natural human activity, is a leading cause of death. These days you can't trust *anybody*. More and more, we're seeing cases where people caught deadly diseases from having sex *with their own selves*. So my advice is, just don't do it, and if you absolutely *must* do it, do it only with somebody you are absolutely certain is reliable, such as a spouse or trusted pet.[21]

5. Avoid accidents. Accidents cause more deaths than any other single thing I intend to mention in this particular sentence. Statistics show that more than 91 percent of all accidents occur either on or off the job, or in the home. So these are three places you should definitely avoid. Driving is also out of the question. Wear a helmet at all times, *especially* when going to the bathroom. Every year more than 650,000 Americans die from head injuries sustained from falling off toilets, yet our so-called "political leaders" do nothing, because they are taking handouts from the powerful commode lobby. Which, for the record, does *not* wash its hands.

6. Get plenty of exercise. Every year, lack of exercise kills more Americans than the Hundred Years War and all the Punic Wars *combined*. So stop sitting around on your giant mesquite-enhanced American butt! No more excuses! I want you to get up RIGHT NOW, walk to the telephone, dial the toll-free number, and order one of those exercise contraptions advertised by hyper-

---

21. I'm just kidding, of course. No WAY should you have sex with your spouse.

enthusiastic spandex-wearing physical freaks on daytime TV in between lawyer commercials. Then you can sit back down—you don't want to overexert yourself on your first day—and allow four to six weeks for delivery. When the device comes, take it out of the box, examine it closely for defects, and—after some basic stretching exercises to loosen up—store it under a bed. Be careful not to strain yourself, lest you sustain a painful back injury and be forced to sue somebody's ass.

8

HOW TO ARGUE WITH YOUR SPOUSE ABOUT MONEY

The Nuclear Option: Tampons

ARGUING IS A NORMAL PART of being married, like finding alien hairs embedded in the bath soap. In any close relationship between two people, there's always going to be a certain amount of friction, sometimes resulting in gunplay.

But when you're arguing, you must keep things in perspective. No matter what particular issue you're arguing about, no matter how serious it seems at the moment, remember that in the long run, the truly important thing—all psychologists agree on this—is that *you must win the argument.* If you win, you receive points that can be redeemed for valuable merchandise at the Marriage Argument Prize Redemption Center.

Not really. The truth is that many marital arguments are complete wastes of time involving idiotically trivial issues. For example, my wife and I routinely argue about what time we need to leave the house. Let's say we're supposed to be at some event that starts at 7 p.m., and that the place where the event is being held is about a 15-minute drive from our house. My wife and I both agree on these basic facts. The problem is that we don't interpret them the same way at all.

- **How I interpret the facts:** I start with the premise that if the event starts at 7 p.m., we need to be physically present at the event at 7 p.m., or, preferably, ten minutes early. Allowing fifteen minutes for the drive, plus ten minutes for finding a parking space, plus another five minutes to walk from the parking space to the event, we need to be in the car, with the engine running, at 6:20 p.m. at the latest. But then I allow a ten-minute cushion in case there is traffic, which pushes it back to 6:10, to which I add another fifteen-minute cushion for the unexpected, such as engine trouble, carjacking, a meteor strike, etc. This now puts our Mandatory Time of Departure (MTD) at 5:55 p.m., or, rounding off, 5:45 p.m. So shortly before then—say, around 5:30—I am ready to go. I am pacing around the house jingling my car keys in a suggestive manner.
- **How my wife interprets the facts:** First off, my wife believes that just because an event is *scheduled* for 7 p.m., that does not mean it will *start* at 7 p.m. Most likely it will start late— 7:15, say, or 7:30—and even then nobody is expected to actually *be* there when it starts, so an arrival time of, say, 8 p.m. is fine. My wife is of Cuban descent, and she be-

lieves this about *all* events, including weddings, funerals, and commercial airplane departures. She also believes in the Special Theory of Automotive Relativity, which holds that when you are traveling inside a car, *there is no passage of time.* You can get into a car at 8 p.m. and drive for 15 minutes, and when you get out of the car, *it will still be 8 p.m.* So if you need to be somewhere at 8, you can leave at 8. Except that my wife will not be ready at 8. She will be ready closer to 8:30, because she will be "running a little late," because it takes her longer than she expected to apply her makeup. It *always* takes her longer than she expected to apply her makeup, but she continues to assume that the next time the process will somehow go quicker, as if one day she'll look into the mirror and discover that she has, I don't know, fewer eyebrows.

So, starting with precisely the same facts, my wife and I arrive at departure times that are three hours apart. This results in tension between us. We resolve it by calmly discussing our differences, then formulating a reasonable and workable compromise.

Seriously, we get into a big honking argument wherein I accuse her of being inconsiderate and out of touch with the known physical laws of the universe, and she accuses me of being a key-jingling time Nazi. If we're in good form, we can make this argument completely ruin any chance of our enjoying the event that we were trying to get to.

Eventually—sometimes several days later, when we can no longer clearly remember what the event *was*—we realize that we're being foolish. We apologize to each other and sincerely promise to do better. And because we are both mature, intelligent adults, the next time we have an event to attend, we have *exactly the same argument.* Tradition is important in a marriage.

Two other topics that married couples traditionally disagree about are child care and housework. Every year, these two areas are the subject of literally millions of marital arguments. And while I certainly would never engage in crude generalizations based on gender, all of these arguments are started by women.

The problem is that women have developed a set of extremely rigid standards concerning child care and housework, and they expect men to meet these standards. Women are not willing to acknowledge that men *also* have standards for child care and housework, but we do. Ours just happen to be *different* standards, as we see in the following chart:

Area of Concern	Women's Standards	Men's Standards
Child Care	You see to it that the children bathe regularly, brush their teeth twice daily, eat three nutritious meals a day, with a minimum of junk food, and wear clean, appropriate clothing. You make sure they receive regular medical and dental care, and that they keep up in school—including homework and special projects. You coordinate their participation in extracurricular activities and sports. At every moment of the day and night, you know exactly where all your children are. When the children are home, you play with them or supervise them in constructive activities. If they are not physically in your presence, you know the name and phone number of the person they are with, and what they are doing. You have memorized the names and phone numbers of the children's doctors, dentists, and teachers.	You feel you have done a good job if, to the best of your knowledge, none of the children are actively bleeding.
Housekeeping	A house is satisfactorily kept when all floors and carpets are vacuumed, all shelves are dusted, and all beds made. In the kitchen, all counters should be wiped, the dishes should be washed and put away, and the refrigerator should be cleaned, with outdated food discarded. All bathroom surfaces should be cleaned, including the shower tile and grout; the toilets should be thoroughly scrubbed with a disinfectant cleanser.	You should be able to find the remote control in under ten minutes.

(chart continues)

Area of Concern	Women's Standards	Men's Standards
Laundry	Dirty clothes should be placed in a hamper. At regular intervals, they should be sorted by color and fabric type, presoaked and/or sprayed with stain remover if necessary, then washed in separate loads at appropriate temperature and time settings, with detergent, softener, and bleach as required. They should then be either placed in the drier at the appropriate setting, or, for delicates, allowed to air-dry. Garments should be ironed as necessary.	For years, you dropped your dirty clothes on the floor, and they wound up coming back clean. But finally one day you got tired of the snide comments from your spouse, plus you needed clean socks, so you took it upon yourself, unasked, to do a load of laundry. With no help from *anyone*, you put all the dirty clothes into the washer, then into the drier, even though it took you several minutes to figure out how to turn these appliances on. You viewed the result as a success, in that your socks did OK. But many of the other garments shrank from normal human sizes to Barbie clothes, plus all the whites came out roughly the color of Hawaiian Punch. Your spouse was highly critical, so you decided never to attempt laundry again, and you resumed dropping your clothes on the floor. So now your spouse has resumed making snide comments. What the hell does she *want*?

(chart continues)

As this chart shows, we men *do* have standards for child care and housework. We would appreciate it if you women would make an honest effort to see things from *our* perspective for a change, and not get all snitty every time we make some teensy little mistake such as forgetting to feed the children for several days, or accidentally leaving a child behind at a turnpike service

Area of Concern	Women's Standards	Men's Standards
Observing a Child's Birthday	Months before the child's birthday, you select a party date and place. You also select a theme and scour the Internet for theme-appropriate decorations, party favors, etc. You arrange for food and entertainment— a clown, a magician, Barry Manilow, etc. You send out invitations, after carefully reviewing the guest list with the child. On the day of the party itself, you turn into a raving theme-crazed lunatic,[22] barking orders to your spouse such as: "I don't care if it's raining, you need to PUT OUT THE YELLOW BRICK ROAD *RIGHT NOW*." At the end of the party, when your house is a child-devastation zone with partially eaten chicken nuggets strewn everywhere, you say, "Wasn't that GREAT??" Then, after a break of about fifteen minutes, you start planning next year's party.	Roughly a month after the child's birth date, you remark: "Hey, doesn't [*name of child*] have a birthday coming up?"

plaza. On behalf of all men everywhere, I ask you women to please cut us a little slack, OK? Also, would you mind fixing us a sandwich? We're hungry! Thanks!

Now that we've dealt with child care and housework, let's tackle the issue that *really* causes trouble in marriages: money. Married couples argue about money more than any other topic.

---

22. I refer here specifically to my wife.

In fact, they usually start arguing about it before they're actually married, when they are planning their wedding.

When I say "they" in the previous sentence, I am of course referring to the bride-to-be and her mother, since they are the ones who plan the wedding. As a rule, the groom-to-be has nothing to do with it. Sometimes the groom-to-be doesn't even know he's getting married until the bride-to-be orders him to rent formal wear. At that point the bride-to-be and her mom have spent *months* poring over bridal magazines the size of meat lockers and talking to wedding planners, printers, florists, caterers, banquet managers, bandleaders, dressmakers, photographers, videographers, jewelers, cake makers, confectioners, and so on, making the thousands of critical decisions necessary to stage a modern American wedding, which involves the same amount of planning as the Normandy Invasion, although of course the wedding is far more expensive.

Eventually two facts penetrate the brain of the groom-to-be: (1) he really and truly is going to get married, and (2) the wedding is going to cost more money than either he or the bride-to-be has ever spent on anything. This strikes the groom-to-be as insane. If he truly believes that he is an equal partner in the relationship, and he is also a complete idiot, he voices this opinion to the bride-to-be.

This is when they have their first big money-related argument. The bride-to-be's position is that their wedding is the culmination of all her girlhood dreams and the sacred public declaration of their love for, and eternal commitment to, each other. The groom-to-be's position is that it is basically a big party requiring uncomfortable rented clothing. He will point out that if they took the wedding money and instead invested it in the stock market, it could pay for their children's college educations. Of course, if the groom-to-be actually *had* the wedding money, he would not invest it in the stock market; he would invest it in a motorcycle. But that's irrelevant, because the groom-to-be never wins this argument. The bride-to-be always wins, because she employs a powerful, persuasive, and logical argument: crying.[23]

So they have a lavish wedding, and it is a wonderful affair documented for posterity by a riveting, professionally produced three-hour video that nobody except the bride and her mother is able to watch for more than ninety seconds without lapsing into a coma. But the pattern has been set: Just as men and women have different standards for child care and housework, they have different priorities about how to spend money.

WOMEN'S TOP TEN FINANCIAL PRIORITIES

1. Shoes
2. Food
3. Shoes
4. Clothing
5. Shoes that go with the clothing
6. Shelter, defined as "a place to keep shoes"
7. Jewelry
8. Shoes that go with the jewelry

---

23. Women have a weapon that is even more effective in arguments against men than crying: tampons. Really. If a woman, in any argument, on any topic, manages to work tampons in—as in, "I don't even have enough money to buy tampons!"—she will win the argument. The man will agree to anything to make her stop talking about tampons. I probably should not reveal this, but men are terrified of tampons. The ultimate horror movie, for men, would be called The Night of the Tampon, and it would feature a man in a big spooky old house, where he is being stalked by a giant vengeful tampon.

9. Saving for the future
10. Shoes that will look good in the future

MEN'S TOP TEN FINANCIAL PRIORITIES

1. A motorcycle

Obviously, with these differing priorities, unless the couple has access to an unlimited amount of money and closet space, there will be conflicts over spending. And if these conflicts are not resolved, they can grow and fester, eventually forming lesions that develop into pustules with circular pores, through which masses of spores are released.

No! Wait! Those are the symptoms of Asian soybean rust, a disease that, according to the American Soybean Association, "has the potential to very negatively affect the U.S. soybean industry . . . with possible yield losses of up to 80 percent or more."

But we cannot concern ourselves with that now. We have to figure out how you married couples out there can resolve your disputes about money. The key is being willing to compromise. Here's an example of what I mean:

Let's say a couple has been trying, with no success, to save money for a down payment on a house. One day the husband discovers that his wife has purchased a $137 pair of shoes that, as far as he can detect with his naked husband eye, are identical to a pair of shoes she bought the previous month. He confronts her about this. She points out that (1) the new shoes are not even remotely identical to the other shoes, which are a *completely different* shade of lime green; and (2) the husband just purchased a new cellular phone, despite the fact that the one he had was only four months old and worked fine. He replies that he needs the new phone because it has "Bluetooth," as well as *both* "EDGE" *and* "GPRS." She asks why he needs these features, and he becomes quite testy, because (1) he dislikes being second-guessed; and (2) he has no idea what these features actually are. He just thought they sounded cool.

So now the couple is having a full-blown money argument. If they allow the situation to deteriorate, their marriage could be in real trouble. This is why they need to compromise—to find a solution that allows *both* of them to feel that their needs are being met. In this case, the ideal compromise would be as follows:

- **THE WIFE** stomps out of the house in a blind rage and charges sixteen dozen pairs of designer shoes, running up an enormous credit card bill and thereby giving . . .
- **THE HUSBAND** the excuse he needs to take out a loan and buy a motorcycle.

Thus we see that, thanks to the power of compromise, what could have been an unproductive spat becomes a "win-win" situation, at least until large men come to take away all their possessions. But no matter what particular financial problems you're having at the moment, you must always remember that marriage is a serious lifetime commitment, often lasting as long as eighteen months. You should also keep in mind that, according to the American Soybean Association, Asian soybean rust spores can remain viable for as long as fifty days.

9

TEACHING YOUR CHILDREN
ABOUT MONEY

Let the Little Bastards Starve

F YOU'RE A PARENT, one of your most important jobs is teaching your children about money. Of course, you also need to teach them about sex, but that's easy: You just sit them down and say, "Children, sex is a very, very important topic. Ask your mother about it."

Teaching kids about money is not so simple, and yet it is vital. As a boy, I learned about money from my dad, who was a Presbyterian minister. The most important lesson I learned from him was: If you want to have money, you should not be a Presbyterian minister.

I'm not saying we were dirt poor. We had plenty of dirt. We were more what I would call "really bad car" poor. We never had a new car, of course, but my dad couldn't even afford a *used* car built by a normal car company such as Ford or Chevrolet. Our cars were built by companies that obviously had more experience making nonautomotive products—toaster ovens, maybe, or salt-water taffy. Apparently one day, the corporate executives, while sitting around a large conference table, decided to branch out from kitchen appliances or candy and take a stab at making— why not?—automobiles. Having no idea what they were doing, they produced these truly awful cars, these turdmobiles, which never achieved market success because nobody would buy them, except, of course, my dad.

For example, we were the only American family that I know of ever to own a Hillman Minx. This was a British car that was engineered in accordance with the philosophy "For maximum passenger safety, the best car is the car that cannot, physically, be started."

You know in movies, when they have a scene where a woman is trying to get away from a scary bad guy, and she jumps into her car and turns the key, and as the bad guy gets closer and closer the starter motor goes *rrr-rrr-rrrr* but the engine won't start? In those scenes, the part of the car is usually played by a Hillman Minx wearing heavy makeup to appear to be some other brand of car. Hollywood professionals have learned that the Minx is the only car that can absolutely be relied upon, when the chips are down, to not start. My boyhood memories of family car trips involve all of us sitting in the car, ready to go somewhere, listening to the familiar sounds of the Minx going *rrr-rrr-rrrr* and my dad saying non-Presbyterian words.

This was actually a good thing, because the Minx also had a feature—at least ours did—whereby the steering wheel would spontaneously become disconnected from the wheels it was supposed to be steering. This happened several times to our Minx, leaving my dad spinning the wheel frantically around and around, like a pretend steering wheel on an amusement-park kiddy ride, while the Minx continued happily onward in whatever direction it had been going. This could have been very dangerous in a different car, but fortunately the Minx—this was another safety feature—

had an engine that, on those rare occasions when it was running, produced approximately the same horsepower as a deceased gerbil, so we were rarely moving faster than 8 miles per hour when the Random-Steering-Disconnect Feature kicked in.

My dad finally got rid of the Minx. That was the good news. The bad news was that he replaced it—just when I got old enough to drive—with a used Nash Metropolitan. This was one of the silliest-looking cars ever made, as we can see from this advertisement for it:

This is not a car designed for grown-ups. This is a car designed to be the lead character in a children's cartoon book entitled *Curtis the Car Goes to the Circus.* In addition to looking silly, the Metropolitan was also ludicrously small, as we can see in these actual photographs of a Metropolitan side by side with actor Tom Cruise and a standard coffeemaker:

From left: **Nash Metropolitan, Tom Cruise, coffeemaker**
(*all images shown actual size*).

The first time I ever drove my own self to pick up an actual girl on an actual date, I was at the wheel of the Metropolitan. I was already insecure and self-conscious enough without having to show up at my date's house driving a vehicle that could easily have been stolen by squirrels.

It did not help that my dad cut my hair. This was another way my family saved money. Dad got a cheap electric hair trimmer from the drugstore, and every two weeks he would give haircuts to me and my brothers. My dad went bald early—somewhere around age seventeen, to judge from the old photos of him—so he was not what you would call keenly sensitive to hairstyles. He put one of those depth guards on the clippers and styled us using the lawn-mower technique, the goal being to get all the hairs, regardless of their location on a person's head, to be a uniform length of about three sixteenths of an inch. It's a fine hairstyle for tennis balls, motel carpeting, certain varieties of coconut, and Eminem, but it doesn't look good on humans. Here's a photo of my dad cutting my hair:

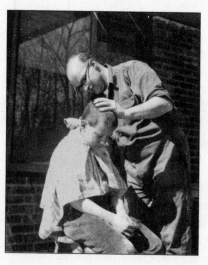

SOURCE:
Matthew Brady

There are a couple of things worth noting in this picture. One is that I am displaying the cheerful, upbeat body language of a prisoner about to be beheaded. The other is that I have a high forehead. Not as high as my dad's forehead—which went all the way over the top of his head and down the back to his shirt collar—but still quite high. So, as you can imagine, I looked really terrific with the tennis-ball hairstyle. To get an idea of *how* terrific I looked, take a gander at this photograph of me in the early sixties, lounging on our living-room sofa in all my coolness with my cool "Hair by My Dad" hairstyle and my equally cool Soviet Union–style eyeglasses from the optical department at Macy's in White Plains:

SOURCE:
Annie Leibovitz

Note that, in addition to the excellent hairstyle and suave eyewear, I am wearing *loafers without socks*. How cool is THAT? You can imagine the impression I made on my date when I pulled up, looking like this, at the wheel of the Nash Metropolitan, ready to head out for a "night on the town" complete with oncoming cars crashing because their drivers were blinded by the glare of their headlights reflecting off my forehead.

I am not asking for your pity here. I had wonderful parents and a fine childhood. I'm just saying that we did not have much money in our household.

This was a good thing, because it taught me that, if I wanted something, I had to work for it. My primary source of income was mowing lawns. When springtime came and the grass started sprouting in our neighborhood, I'd go out to the shed and get out our lawn mower. I'd spend the next two hours yanking on the starter rope, which was a complete waste of time because we had (needless to say) a used lawn mower that was obviously designed by the same crack engineers responsible for the Hillman Minx. It was no more capable of internal combustion than a zucchini. Eventually I would give up, go inside, and beg my parents for money, and they'd give me some. Yes, it was hard work. But I learned the value of a dollar.

Now let's fast-forward several decades to the current generation of young people, the generation that was produced by me and my fellow Baby Boomers. There has been a lot of criticism about us Boomers, but I think we can say in all modesty that, despite our flaws in other areas, when it comes to parenting, we have done a truly horrible job. In an effort to make life perfect for our children, we have ruined them. Instead of teaching them that they have to work for nice things, we've simply *given* them everything—money, clothes, computers, phones, TVs, travel, cars, college educations, and, most damaging of all, lawn mowers that start instantly. We have raised a generation of young people who believe they're the center of the universe. This is sick and twisted. WE'RE the center of the universe!

No, wait, what I mean is, we Boomers have raised a generation of kids who expect their parents to provide everything for them, even after they become adults. This has led to the so-called "boomerang generation" phenomenon, wherein young people graduate from college and then—instead of going the traditional young-graduate route of getting a crappy job and living in a crappy apartment furnished largely with anti-roach devices—they *move back in with their parents.*

This is just WRONG. This is AGAINST NATURE. This is like a fully grown 200-pound adult kangaroo climbing back into its mother's pouch. We Boomers engaged in some shameful activities—indiscriminate drug use, the attempted overthrow of the U.S. government, disco—but *we did not move back in with our parents.* In fact, this may be our single greatest achievement, as a generation.

Generational Comparison

Name of Generation	Major Accomplishments
The "Greatest Generation"	• Overcame the brutal hardships of the Great Depression • Won World War II • Made the U.S. the most prosperous and powerful nation in world history
The Baby Boomers	• Did not move back in with our parents

If you're a parent with a child in college, you need to take steps to prevent the child from moving back in with you. One excellent way is for you and your spouse to start walking around the house naked. It's also a good idea to convert the child's bedroom to a space that is less than ideal for human habitation, such as a racquetball court, walk-in freezer, python cage, or plutonium-storage vault. Another good idea is to tell your child: "You're welcome to move back in with us, under one condition: *Dad will cut your hair.*"

If, despite these measures, your child still intends to move back in with you, you must sell your house, move, and assume a new identity. Currently, 78 percent of the people in the federal Witness Protection Program are parents hiding out from children attempting to boomerang on them.

But the best way to avoid this problem is to raise your child with the right attitude about money. Here's how:

Start When the Child Is Young

When I say "young," I mean, "while the child is still in the delivery room." Be firm! Just because a newborn child is crying out to be fed, that does *not* mean you should automatically stick a breast into his mouth. This causes the child to get used to instant gratification, which means that when he grows up, he'll think that whenever things don't work out exactly the way he wants them to, the solution is to stick a breast into his mouth. This is probably what happened to me.

You should also encourage children to be self-reliant and do things for themselves. At the age of two months, Donald Trump was changing his own diapers.[24]

Give the Child a Fair Allowance

What is a fair allowance? The answer depends on many factors, by which I mean: three dollars a week. That's *plenty*. This allowance will teach your children the importance of financial discipline and saving to buy things that he wants. Suppose, for example, that your child really wants a computer that costs $1,395. Explain to the child that if he can save just one dollar each week out of his allowance, he'll be able to buy the computer in only 1,395 weeks,

---

24. He still is today!

or just a little under twenty-seven years! At this point the child may want to stick a breast into his mouth, but *don't let him*.

Never allow a child to spend all of his allowance. Insist that he set aside a certain amount of money every week and put it in a safe place, where you can get it if you need to buy beer.

Encourage the Child to Develop an Entrepreneurial Spirit

Many children learn about money by starting their own businesses, the classic example being the sidewalk lemonade stand. This is an opportunity to teach your child fundamental economic principles. I'm not suggesting that you encourage your child to have a lemonade stand; that's WAY too much work. I'm suggesting that you explain to your child that if he buys lemonade from some *other* kid's stand, and then happens to choke on a lemon seed, then you would be in a position to sue the other kid's parents for thousands of dollars. *That* is what I mean by "fundamental economic principles."

But whatever else you teach your child, the most important lesson that you, as a parent, can impart is that *money is not everything*. There are more important things in life than money—things like spirituality, knowledge, friendship, and, above all, family. *These* are the things that truly bring happiness.

So, on second thought, two dollars a week is plenty.

10

PROVIDING FOR YOUR
CHILDREN'S COLLEGE
EDUCATIONS

The Hell with It

THE MOST PRECIOUS GIFT that a parent can give to a child—more precious than material things such as diamonds, or gold, or a big mansion—is a big mansion filled with diamonds and gold.

Alas, most of us cannot afford to give this to our children, so we must settle for sending them to college. We're giving them the gift of knowledge, which is also precious, especially in these modern "high-tech" times. Take computers. Today, if you don't know how to operate a computer,[25] you're limiting yourself to a lifetime of manual labor in a boring, menial, "dead-end" job such as professional golfer or porn star. Whereas, if you can operate a computer,

---

25. In case you don't know, here's how to operate a computer: (1) Turn it on. (2) Wait for it to "boot up." (3) Call "Technical Support."

chances are that you will become an employee of a large corporation that will let you have *your very own cubicle space,* where you may be permitted to put up small photographs of your children or dog until such time as your job is outsourced to Kuala Lumpur.

This is the gift that you give when you give your child a college education. Unfortunately, college costs money, unless your child is really good at football or basketball, in which case good-hearted knowledge-loving strangers will cover all your child's educational needs, including a sport utility vehicle.

But chances are you'll have to pay for your child's college education. This is a problem if your child wants to go to a top college such as Harvard, where tuition is currently $37,500 per . . .

. . . no, wait, while I was writing that sentence it went up, so now it's $38,928 per . . .

. . . no, hold on, it just went up again, and now it's $40,2 . . .

OK, never mind. There is simply no way, using currently available technology, to keep track of the rising cost of sending a child to Harvard or other Ivy League school. Why are Ivy League schools so expensive? Simple: They hire the smartest professors in the world, and these professors do nothing[26] but sit around thinking up ways to jack up tuition.

The pioneer in this effort was Princeton University, which in 1932 hired Albert Einstein to work on the tuition problem. At the time, a semester at Princeton cost $16.75, which included a class beanie and a manservant. After studying the situation, Einstein developed the General Theory of Relativity, which states: "People in general will pay any amount of money to be able to tell their relatives that their child goes to Princeton."

---

26. The actual classes are taught by graduate students making $9.50 an hour.

This remains the fundamental underlying economic principle behind Ivy League tuitions. Researchers at Yale, using a super-computer, recently concluded that there is "theoretically no upper limit" to how much parents are willing to pay to send their children to an Ivy League school. Dartmouth seems to be proving this with its Tuition + Organ Program (TOP), which requires that each semester's tuition payment be accompanied by a functional human kidney.

"It's amazing," reports a Dartmouth official. "We figured that, between Mom and Dad, each set of parents would be good for a maximum of four kidneys, but darned if they're not coming up with more! God only knows how."

And that's what's going on *today*. The situation is only going to get worse. Let's say you have a child in kindergarten now. By the time that child enters college, at the rate things are going, he or she will have tattoos the size of doormats. Also tuition will be really high.

So we know that sending your child to a good school will cost a lot of money. What does this mean? It means that, as a responsible parent, you need to start planning *now*. I don't mean planning how to pay for a good college: I mean planning how to get your child to go to a mediocre or actively bad college.

Your best bet, of course, is low grades. A child with a crappy grade-point average is almost guaranteed not to get into a good school. But bad grades don't just happen by themselves. You need to closely monitor your child's study habits and set strict guidelines. ("There will be no studying until after you've watched your five hours of television, young man!")

You must also be alert for subtle signs that your child is secretly becoming involved in academics, such as:

- Hiding books under the mattress
- Using big words such as "curriculum" and "dormitory"
- Hanging around with friends who make eye contact with you and speak in complete sentences
- Disappearing from the house for hours at a time, "coincidentally" on school days

You have to watch your child like a hawk, because these young people can be very sneaky. In one chilling case, a mother—a mother who held the confident belief, based on all outward evidence, that her son was a complete loser—happened to look in his closet, and to her horror found not only applications to MIT and Stanford but also a working cold-fusion nuclear reactor. Fortunately, before this woman and her husband were forced to pay hundreds of thousands of dollars in tuition, they were able to stage an intervention, which involved forcing their son to play video games while listening to hip-hop music for eighty straight hours. Difficult?[27] Yes. But it paid off: Today that same young man is working as an assistant night manager at a Wendy's.

OK, let's say that, thanks to strict parental discipline and hard work, you have positioned your child to attend a mediocre, low-prestige college with reasonable tuition rates. The question now becomes: *Which* low-prestige college should your child attend? And how can you be *sure* it's mediocre? Here are some factors you need to consider, in order of importance:

1. Length of college name. The longer the name, the more mediocre and reasonably priced the college is likely to be. Thus you want to avoid colleges with names like "Smith" or

---

27. Have you noticed that I ask a lot of rhetorical questions? Don't answer this.

"Brown," and look instead at colleges with names like "The Earl T. Bunderson Greater Tri-City Area Community College of Agricultural, Commercial, Industrial, and Pharmaceutical Arts and Applied Dental Hygiene and Waste Management Sciences." You should also beware of colleges with lengthy applications that ask suspicious questions like where your child went to high school, and what his or her grades were. You're looking for a college with a one-page application devoted almost entirely to explaining how you can pay by major credit card.

2. Mascot. The good college mascot names were taken long ago by old established schools, which tend to have higher tuitions. To find a school in your price range, look for a mascot along the lines of "The Fighting Sphincters."

3. Parking. Parking is the single biggest crisis facing American higher education today. Despite the fact that colleges are, theoretically, institutions of higher learning, it apparently has never occurred to the geniuses who run them that anybody would be arriving by car. The result is that most colleges have approximately one parking space per 150 students, which means that many students spend their entire college careers cruising around looking for a legal spot. Many students are forced to park illegally and receive parking tickets, which at your top Ivy League schools can cost $5,000 per violation. So when you and your child interview at a prospective college, be sure to ask the interviewer probing questions such as: "How many parking spaces does this college have?" "Where do *you* park?" "Can my child park in your space when you're not conducting interviews?"

4. Social life. College is not just about parking. College is also a place where young people make the transition from immaturity to adulthood via a process of forming long-term social bonds with other young people and then, later in the evening, getting drunk and possibly dropping large objects such as pianos off the roofs of tall buildings. This process occurs most readily at colleges with an active fraternity and sorority system. To determine whether a specific college has an active Greek system, visit the campus on a Saturday night and look for badly maintained buildings with large Greek letters painted on them and young men urinating out the windows.

5. Access to cheap Mexican food. All colleges within the continental United States must be located within 50 yards of a cheap Mexican restaurant containing active bacteria colonies dating back to the Reagan Administration. This is federal law. Also, all trees and lampposts within a radius of one mile of the campus must be covered with faded flyers advertising performances six months ago by bands with names like Thunder Meat.

6. Courses. Many colleges also offer courses, wherein students sit in a classroom once or twice a week and exchange e-mails while a graduate assistant drones away about some topic. You want your child to take courses that can lead to getting an actual job after graduation. This means you need to steer your child away from "liberal arts" and "humanities" courses involving nonbusiness topics such as humanity. If your child expresses an interest in, say, Shakespeare, or Aristotle, you must sit your child down and explain that, in the modern corporate environment, nobody cares about these guys, because they have both been dead for like 150 years. What you need in the modern corporate environment is up-to-date business information, such as the phone number for Technical Support. So your child should take only those courses that teach practical business knowledge, courses with titles like Business Administration, Marketing, Accounting, Business Communications, Marketing to Accountants, Administering a Communications Business, Communicating with Marketing Administrators, Cubicle Hygiene, Adjusting the Crappy Office Chair They Give You, and How to Steal a Co-worker's Stapler After Somebody Steals Yours.

Armed with this practical information, your child will be ready to go out and get a paying job in the modern corporate environment, as opposed to moving back in with you. Just to be sure, it's a good idea, as a motivational tool, to move to another state just before graduation without telling your child your new address. Don't worry about your child: This is a great country with a great economy, and there are tons of money-making opportunities out there. Such as selling kidneys to Dartmouth parents.

11

STARTING YOUR OWN BUSINESS

Harness the Awesome Power of Human Stupidity

CONSIDER THE FOLLOWING PEOPLE: John D. Rockefeller. Thomas Edison. Henry Ford. Irving Chevrolet. General Electric. What do they have in common?

Correct: They are all dead. But before they died, they got really rich. And do you know why? *They started their own businesses.*

Why can't you do the same thing? Why shouldn't *you* benefit from your talents?

One reason, of course, is that you don't really have any talent. But that shouldn't stop you any more than it stopped Paris Hilton. All you need is *one idea,* and you could make it big! And the beautiful thing is, it doesn't even have to be a *good* idea. People have gotten rich from business concepts that seemed, at first glance, insanely stupid.

Consider bottled water. Back in the 1950s, when dinosaurs roamed the earth and I was growing up, there was no such thing as bottled water. We drank the water that came out of the faucet, or from water fountains, which were everywhere. We viewed water as an abundant commodity that was widely available in the form of streams, rivers, lakes, glaciers, and rainfall, which came directly out of the sky at no charge. In fact, *all* of this water was free, and it seemed to get the job done, in the sense of being wet. Back then, if you had said, "I'm going to put water into little plastic bottles and try to sell these bottles at a price *higher,* per fluid ounce, than the price of beer," people would have laughed at you and blown cigarette smoke in your face, because back then everybody smoked, including household pets.

But today, bottled water is a billion-dollar industry. We are awash in it. In the future, archeologists digging on the North American continent will discover the remains of our civilization under a 1,000-foot-thick layer of discarded Dasani bottles.

Millions and millions of people simply refuse to drink any water that does not come from a plastic bottle. The bottled-water industry, through shrewd marketing, has convinced all these people that bottled water is healthier and cleaner than regular water. But is this true? Take a look at this bottle of water:

To your naked eye, the water looks pure and clean and wholesome, right? But when we take a sample drop from this very bottle and magnify it 10,000 times under a laboratory microscope, we discover that it contains many impurities:

Impurities Found in a Single Drop of Bottled Water

SOURCE: *Consumer Reports*

Does this mean that you should not drink bottled water? Of course not! It simply means that bottled water contains many hideous things that can kill you.

But that is not the point. The point is that an idea that seemed totally crazy when it was first proposed ended up making a lot of money.

Another good example is "reality" television. Years ago, nobody would have believed that millions of Americans would tune in, week after week, to watch attention-seeking dimwits degrade themselves on shows with names like *Who Wants to Marry Their First Cousin?* But guess what. The producers of these shows are getting *rich*. And that is why we must track them down and kill them.

No, that would be wrong, and possibly illegal. The truth is that "reality" shows, like bottled water, teach us an important business lesson, a lesson that is both inspirational and heartwarming: People are unbelievably stupid. You can get them to buy *anything*, if you market it right.

So you need to come up with an idea for a business. You want to start by deciding on a target demographic of people who (a) have money, and (b) would be willing to give you some. A prime target, in the sense of having more money than it can spend intelligently, is:

Baby Boomers

There are millions of us Boomers, and we have money, and we are needy, needy, needy. We need *everything*. For example, we were the first generation that needed to take ten weeks of night classes to learn how to have babies, which humans had previously been doing for thousands of generations with no formal training whatsoever.

And now that we Boomers are getting old, we need more services than ever. For example, I need somebody to tell me where my reading glasses are. Like many Boomers, I own somewhere in the neighborhood of four hundred pairs of cheap reading glasses, and at any given moment I cannot find any of them. You could start a business for people like me called: Where the Hell Are My Reading Glasses? You would charge us, say, $9.95 a month, and whenever we lost our glasses, we would call you up, and you would tell us where they are. And if you're wondering how you would know where our glasses were, the answer is that you wouldn't *have* to know, because we would also forget where we put your phone number. While we were looking around for it, we'd step on something sharp, and that would be our reading glasses.

Another potentially big moneymaker would be to start a medical clinic for aging Boomer guys. Most of us older guys know we should see our doctors more often, but we are reluctant to do so because the doctor always wants to check our prostate gland, which is an organ located inside guys somewhere around the tonsils, to judge from how far the doctor reaches in there to get to it using a technique that I will not describe in detail here, other than to say that it makes you never want to shake hands with a doctor again.

So I see a huge profit potential in a chain of medical centers for aging Boomer guys called Touchless Health Care. These would be based on the concept of the "brushless" car wash, where no brush comes into physical contact with the car. The examination rooms at Touchless Health Care would be large, maybe 75 yards across. You, the aging guy patient, would stand on one side of the room; the physician would stand on the other side and conduct the examination via binoculars.

"LOOKS GOOD FROM HERE," the physician would shout.

Note: Guys who felt that this procedure was too invasive would have the option of undergoing this examination without binoculars.

Another service business you could start is Technical Support for Boomers. We Boomers are having a lot of trouble with technology these days, particularly if the technology is "digital." Oh, we know that digital is good. Everybody tells us this. We know that sooner or later every electrical thing we own, including our toaster, will be digital. We just don't get how digital works.

This is particularly true of digital music. We Boomers come from a predigital era when all music came in a format known, technically, as the "round" format. First you had your records—your 78s, your 45s, your 33s—and then later you had your CDs. But they all worked the same way: You had a round thing that had music on it, and you put this thing onto or into some kind of player that spun it around, and this caused the music to come out of the speakers (also round).

We Boomers were comfortable with this system, because you always knew exactly where your music was: It was on the round thing. And it did not get mixed up: The Beach Boys were on your Beach Boys round thing; the Rolling Stones were on your Rolling Stones round thing; Ray Charles was on the Ray Charles round thing; Barry Manilow was in the Barry Manilow bin back at the record store; and so on.

Today, thanks to "digital" technology, there is no way to tell for sure *where* the hell your music is. It might be on a little tiny chip the size of a toenail that holds 19,000 songs all mixed in there together, which means two things: (1) Satan is clearly involved, and (2) a reasonably strong ant could make off with your entire music collection. Or, instead of a chip, your music might be in an iPod, or some other small, digital, extremely lose-able non-round thing. Or maybe your music is on your computer. Or your cell phone. Or somewhere on the Internet in general. Or—if you have a new model—on your toaster. With digital technology, you're never sure *where* your music is.

This is no problem for today's young people, who emerge from the womb crying digital cries. But it's extremely confusing for those of us who grew up with the round format. At least it is for me, and I'm sure it is for millions of others like me. That's where Technical Support for Boomers would come in. It would be a number you'd call for technical support, but with an important difference: *The people answering the phone would be as old as the people calling.* This would eliminate the problem with most "technical support" people, who are 24.3 years old, which means that, in order for you to understand what they're telling you, you have to already know enough technical stuff that you would never need to call Technical Support in the first place. When I call Technical Support, I always have conversations like this:

SUPPORT PERSON: How can I help you?

ME: OK, I have this Vortex SoundLoin music player thingie my kids gave me for Father's Day, and I'm trying to figure out how to play a song on it. I *think* I have it turned on, but I'm not sure. I definitely pushed all the buttons, but nothing seems to be happening. At least, I don't . . .

SUPPORT PERSON (*interrupting*): Can you tell me what music format you're using?

ME: Format?

SUPPORT PERSON (*sighing*): The music format.

ME: Oh. Motown.

SUPPORT PERSON: Excuse me?

ME: "Chain of Fools" by Aretha Franklin. OK, technically she didn't *record* it for Motown, but her genre was definitely . . .

SUPPORT PERSON (*interrupting*): No, I mean what *digital* format. MP3? WMA? WAV?

ME:

SUPPORT PERSON: Hello?

ME (*sheepishly*): I don't know my format.

SUPPORT PERSON (*sighing*): Can you tell me the serial number of the unit? It's a 63-digit number that should begin with either EX93857 or EX93957.

ME (*squinting*): I don't see anything like that. You don't happen to know where my reading glasses are, do you? Ha ha!

SUPPORT PERSON:

ME: OK, really, I can't find the serial number.

SUPPORT PERSON: It's on the bottom.

ME (*squinting*): Which side is the bottom?

SUPPORT PERSON (*sighing*): The side where you insert the batteries.

ME: It takes batteries?

So I usually come out of the Technical Support experience without a solution to my technical problem, and, as a bonus, I feel like a moron. This is why I believe Technical Support for Boomers would be a terrific business. Instead of some sighing whipper-snapper, you would talk to a person your own age, who would be sympathetic to your specific technical abilities and needs:

SUPPORT PERSON: How can I help you?

ME: OK, I have this Vortex SoundLoin music player thingie my kids gave me for Father's Day, and I'm trying to figure out how to play a song on it. I *think* I have it turned on, but I'm not sure. I definitely pushed all the buttons, but nothing seems to be happening. At least, I don't *think* anything is.

SUPPORT PERSON: I hate it when that happens! Why do there have to be so many buttons anyway?

ME: Exactly!

SUPPORT PERSON: OK, so you're saying it's a music player?

ME: Yes, and I can't get any music to come out.

SUPPORT PERSON: Huh! I think sometimes, with these new ones, before you get the music out, you have to put the music *in* there.

ME: Really? How?

SUPPORT PERSON: Well, I can't say for sure without my reading glasses, but I think you have to use a computer.

ME: Oh God.

SUPPORT PERSON: I know! It's crazy!

ME: All I want to do is listen to this one song, "Chain of Fools."

SUPPORT PERSON: Aretha!

ME: Yes!

SUPPORT PERSON: I love that song! (*Singing*). "My father said, 'Come on home . . .' "

SUPPORT PERSON AND ME SINGING TOGETHER: "My doctor said, 'Take it eeeeeeeeEEEEEASY . . .' "

ME: Damn, that woman can sing.

SUPPORT PERSON: I *know*. You hear these women singers today, like whatshername . . .

ME: The one with the cleavage?

SUPPORT PERSON: Yes! What *is* her name?

ME: I don't remember. But she has no talent.

SUPPORT PERSON: I know! Take away her cleavage, she's nothing.

ME: She's selling Frappucinos at Starbucks.

SUPPORT PERSON: Aretha has talent *and* cleavage.

ME: Oh God yes. You could lose a backhoe in there.

SUPPORT PERSON: Try telling *that* to these kids today.

ME: Isn't *that* the truth. Well, listen, I'm sure you have other people waiting. Thanks so much for the help!

SUPPORT PERSON: It's why I am here.

Wouldn't that be a great service? Granted, you won't solve your technical problem, but let's face it, you'll never solve it anyway. The reason your kids gave you the music player in the first place was that they knew eventually you'd give up on learning how to use it and give it to them.

But the point is that Technical Support for Boomers could be a very successful business. And not just because of digital music. There's also the whole issue of digital photos. There are millions of Boomers out there taking pictures with digital cameras, and the majority of them *do not know how to get the picture out of the camera*. The only way they can see their pictures now is on the little screen on the camera itself, which means when they get home from their once-in-a-lifetime trip to the Grand Canyon, their visual souvenir of one of nature's most spectacular and majestic vistas looks like this:

A person frustrated by digital photography would definitely benefit from Technical Support for Boomers, which would offer timely and specific advice ("What I do is buy postcards").

I've given you some good Boomer-related ideas. But the truth is that *any* business you come up with that targets Baby Boomers will probably be a big success. You don't even necessarily have to have a real business. You could just select Boomers at random from the phone book and send them invoices for "services rendered," and a lot of us Boomers would pay them. We'd just assume you had provided some service to us, and we forgot what it was.

Speaking of cluelessness, another prime target demographic group for your business could be:

Pet Owners

It is a known fact that modern pet owners are completely insane. There was a time when dogs and cats were considered to be, basically, dogs and cats. We were very *fond* of them, of course, but we understood that they were animals, and we did not confuse animals with humans, except sometimes late at night in parts of the South.

That line has long since been crossed. Many modern pet owners consider their pets to be *much* more important than the actual humans in their lives. These pet owners will cheerfully pay for any service or product that they believe will make their pet happier, including gourmet pet food, spa treatments, trust funds, plastic surgery, designer clothes, footwear, physical therapists, psychologists and—I am not making this up—pet psychics. That is correct: There are people out there who will pay somebody good money to *tell them what their dog is thinking.* Let me just say, as a person who has owned a number of dogs: If you can't figure out what a dog is thinking, you are, with all due respect, dumber than ketchup. Without even knowing your specific dog, I can tell you right now what it's thinking. It's thinking one of the Ten Basic Dog Thoughts.

THE TEN BASIC DOG THOUGHTS

1. "Bark!"
2. "Time to eat!"
3. "Bark! Bark!"
4. "Here's an object! I'd better pee on it!"
5. "Or have sex with it!"
6. "Bark Bark! Bark!"
7. "Mmmm! Crotch!"
8. "Time to eat again!"
9. "Bark! Bark! Bark! Bark!
10. "Barkbarkbarkbarkbarkbarkbarkbarkbarkbarkbarkbarkbark-barkbarkbarkbarkbarkbarkbarkbarkbarkbarkbarkbarkbark-barkbarkbarkbarkbarkbarkbarkbarkbarkbarkbarkbarkbark-barkbarkbarkbarkbarkbarkbarkbarkbarkbarkbarkbarkbark-barkbarkbarkbarkbarkbarkbarkbarkbarkbarkbarkbarkbark-barkbarkbarkbarkbarkbarkbarkbarkbarkbarkbarkbarkbark!"

SOURCE: PETA

If you can come up with a product or service that pet owners will think their pets need or want, you *will* get rich. One idea I had, which you are welcome to use, is: Dead Squirrels by Mail. There are few things in the world that make a dog happier than getting hold of a squirrel, and yet very few dogs ever get to enjoy this pleasure, because the brain of a standard squirrel is nearly one molecule in diameter, which means squirrels seriously out-class dogs in the tactical thinking department. Go to any park, and you will see dogs racing around at top speed, nearly insane with frustration, ramming headfirst into trees at speeds upwards of 30 miles per hour in their fruitless efforts to catch squirrels, while the squirrels themselves are safely up in their trees laughing so hard that the ground beneath them is damp with squirrel drool.[28]

So the idea is, to make these dogs—and of course their own-ers—happy, you would start a business that would, each month, mail your customers a dead squirrel. I guarantee that the arrival of this package would be WAY more exciting for the dog than any dog-spa treatment. There would be urine *everywhere*.

The reason it has to be a dead squirrel, of course, is that if it was alive, it would easily elude the dog. Another possibility would be to mail live squirrels, but hobble them by putting tiny shackles on their paws so the dogs could catch them. The problem there is that the dog might be one of those mutant miniature breeds that look like the result of a biological experiment to see what hap-pens when you mate a gerbil with a ball of lint:

---

28. "Squirrel Drool" would be a good name for a rock band.

Even a hobbled squirrel would take about four seconds to reduce this dog to Purina Squirrel Chow. No, dead squirrels are definitely the way you want to go. Fortunately, there is an abundant supply of them occurring naturally all around you, if you just look.

Another potentially huge moneymaker is cell phones for pets. You know how you often see businesspeople walking around in public talking on those cell-phone headsets, which enable them to harness the awesome power of global communications technology to look like total assholes? It is only a matter of time before pet owners start wanting these things for their pets:

If your pet was wearing a cell phone with a headset, you could always stay in constant contact with it and find out exactly what it was thinking ("barkbarkbarkbarkbark").

Yet another pet-related business you could make big money in is pet cloning. I found out about this from the *New York Times*,[29] which had a story about this person who loved his cat so much

_____

29. A newspaper.

that he was planning to pay a pet-cloning company $32,000 for a new one. That is correct: *$32,000.* For a *cat.* We have to ask ourselves, as a society, what has happened to our priorities and our values when—at a time when many young people in this country cannot afford to go to college—a person is willing to spend, to replace a cat, an amount of money that could be used to buy—and this is a conservative estimate—9,000 gallons of beer.

This is a horrible misuse of resources. You definitely should cash in on it. What you do is start a company called Discount Scientific Pet Cloning. Your competitive edge would be that you'd charge *half* what the "big boys" were charging for pet clones. Here's how your business would work: You'd tell your customers to mail you a photo of their pet, plus a plastic baggie containing some of the pet's DNA, which could be in the form of a hair, a saliva-soaked tennis ball, a tapeworm, a poop, some fabric from a piece of furniture that the pet was fond of attempting to mate with, etc. You would take these items into your Scientific Cloning Laboratory, which would be your garage. There, using a pair of sterile tongs, you would throw the baggie away. Then you would go to an animal shelter and get a replacement pet. This is why you need the photograph: You want the replacement to look at least vaguely like the pet that it is replacing. At the very least you want it to be the same species. Like, if the original pet was a cat, you don't want to be sending the owner a llama. For one thing, llamas are really hard to mail.

Perhaps you are thinking: "Wait a minute: If you're not actually cloning the pets, isn't that . . . *fraud?*" Well, if you want to use a picky legalistic definition of "fraud"—i.e., committing an act of fraud—the answer is, technically, yes. But trust me: Once your customer receives the "cloned" pet, he or she will immediately fall in love with it, because (1) all animals are capable of touching the hearts of humans on a deep emotional level, and (2) your customer is an idiot, which is why he or she is attempting to clone a pet by mail in the first place.

OK, I've given you some practical, "can't miss" business ideas. If you try them, and they work out for you, I ask for nothing in return except for your thanks, and a large amount of money. Also, if you find any reading glasses, those are mine.

12

HOW TO GET RICH IN THE
STOCK MARKET

Or: Not

THE STOCK MARKET, or "Wall Street," is the most prominent symbol of our national wealth, bestriding the American economy, in the words of Walt Whitman, "like some kind of big thing that bestrides something else."

But what, exactly, is the stock market? In technical economic terms, it is a building in New York City where hundreds of excited men and women gather to shout at one another until they have armpit stains the size of catchers' mitts. These people are called "traders," and they are trading "stocks," which are pieces of "paper" that say the "bearer" owns a tiny fraction, or "share," of a company.

For example, if you buy one share of Microsoft, and Microsoft has ten billion shares outstanding, you—even if you are just some dirtbag—*literally own one ten-billionth of Microsoft.* Does this mean you can go to Microsoft headquarters in Redmond, Washington, and exchange your share for, say, a coffeemaker? Of course not. A coffeemaker is three shares.[30] For one share, you get an acoustic ceiling tile.

But the real value of stocks doesn't come from trading them in; it comes from holding on to them while they appreciate in value. For example, suppose that, back in 1950, you had $10 to invest. If you had put that $10 into a bank passbook-savings account at 2 percent compound interest, and you kept it there, today it would be worth, allowing for inflation, $238.62.[31]

Sounds pretty good, right? But if you had taken that same $10 and invested it in IBM stock in 1950, today it would be worth, geez, probably a *lot* of money. Of course you can't *use* this money, because by this point, if you're still alive, you're sitting in a nursing home watching *Wheel of Fortune,* with a streamer of drool from your mouth to your lap, wondering what the hell you did with your teeth.

So, the financial lesson we learn from this example is that you should never leave your money anywhere for *too* long. Your best use of this particular $10 would have been to blow the whole thing on a steak dinner back in 1950, when good steak was cheap and nobody gave a damn about cholesterol.

But getting back to the stock market: It can be a good way to make money, but only if you know what you're doing. You do NOT buy stocks based on the latest fad, or some "hot tip" from your uncle Herb. For one thing, you don't have an uncle Herb. For another thing, the only way to make money in the stock market is to use a rational system, based on solid information, *not*

---

30. **Bill Gates personally has seventeen million coffeemakers.**
31. **I made this number up. I have no idea what "compound interest" is, let alone how to allow for inflation.**

guesswork. The only *proven* way to make money in the market is to follow this three-step procedure:

Step 1: Gather all available financial data on the top one thousand stocks for the past twenty-five years.

Step 2: By conducting a thorough analysis of each stock—taking into consideration its performance against the overall market, splits, price/earnings ratio, earned-run average, etc.—select the ten stocks that have performed best in this time period.

Step 3: Using a time machine, go back twenty-five years and buy these stocks.

This system is pretty much foolproof except for one teensy flaw, which you may have already detected: You are *way* too lazy to do the research. Most people are. This is why most people use stockbrokers.

A stockbroker is a person who has been trained to analyze your personal situation and develop a unique financial strategy that is tailored specifically to your needs and your goals, using the following chart:

Stockbroker Financial-Strategy Decision-Making Chart

Your Specific Situation	Stockbroker's Recommended Financial Strategy
I'm a young person with a modest income, but I'm expecting it to grow. I'm investing for the long haul and willing to take some risks.	*You should definitely buy stocks.*
I'm an older person, nearing retirement and thinking in terms of conserving my "nest egg."	*The wisest course for you would be to invest in the stock market.*
I'm a homeless person with no income, living on Dumpster food and sleeping in a storm drain. I smell like a toilet, and tiny spiders live in my hair.	*If you find any money, bring it in, and we'll put you in low-cost stocks.*
I'm a happily married woman, but I'm attracted to my boss (he's also happily married). Lately we've been spending more and more time together, and I'm afraid something might happen. The problem is on some level, I think I *want* it to.	*Unless you want to destroy what sound like two perfectly good marriages, both you and your boss need to really think about where you're heading, and then buy stocks.*
I'm a vampire.	*We can make special arrangements to sell you stocks at night.*
I just learned that a giant asteroid is going to strike the earth tomorrow, wiping out all human life.	*There are some terrific stock bargains to be had in this type of market.*

As we can see, the unique strategy that the stockbroker is going to tailor for you will involve selling you stocks, because, duh, he's a *stockbroker*. His job is to sell stocks. If he were in the cattle business, trust me, the unique financial strategy he'd tailor for you would involve heifers.

Does this mean that stocks are a bad investment? Not at all! Stocks can be an excellent wealth-building mechanism when they are going up, as we learn by studying the following statistical graph:

But sometimes, stocks go down, as we see here:

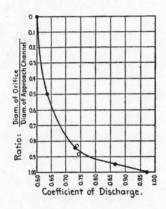

And sometimes stocks seem to be going in both directions at the same time:

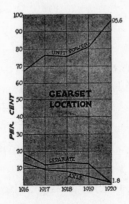

And sometimes there is no way to tell *what* the hell is going on:

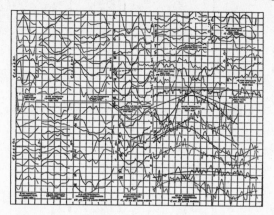

So the "bottom line" is that the stock market is unpredictable. Nobody really has a clue what it's going to do. Oh, sure, there are many stock market "analysts" and "experts." They're on TV all the time, wearing suits and talking in a confident, highly informed manner. But it turns out that their specific area of expertise, in a nutshell, is: the past. They're extremely good at thinking up possible explanations for things that have already happened. If there is one teensy gap in their understanding, that area would be: the future. Here, they are pretty much clueless. That's why those financial shows on TV always sound like this:

HOST: Welcome to *Inside Wall Street from the Inside,* the program where Wall Street insiders, with inside information, give you, the investor, the "inside scoop" on what's *really* going on inside the stock market. Today the Dow Jones Industrial Average fell 13 points, so let's go straight to our panel of insiders and see "what's cooking." John, we'll start with you.

FIRST EXPERT: Well, Bob, I think what we're seeing here is investors reacting to developments in the Middle East.

HOST: What, exactly, were those developments, John?

FIRST EXPERT: Beats the shit out of me, Bob. Foreign affairs are not my specialty; I'm a Wall Street insider. All I know is, they are always having developments over there in the Middle East, and in my inside opinion, investors are reacting to them.

HOST: Mary?

SECOND EXPERT: Bob, I would have to agree with John to a degree, but I think investors are also feeling a deeper sense of unease.

HOST: Over what?

SECOND EXPERT: Oh, I don't know if it's anything *specific*, Bob. Did you ever just wake up, and you felt a sort of, you know, unease? I think that's what's going on with the investors. They're like, "Whoa! I'm uneasy!"

HOST: Norm, do you agree?

THIRD EXPERT: To an extent, yes, Bob. But only to an extent.

HOST: What do you mean?

THIRD EXPERT: I have no earthly idea, Bob.

HOST: All right, then. Now let's ask our Wall Street insiders to "put on their prognostication caps" and give us their assessment of what we can expect to see from the market in the coming days and weeks. John?

FIRST EXPERT: Bob, I look for the market to continue to experience downward pressures. But by the same token we could very well see some trends that could tend to exert countervailing pressures. Which of these factors will dominate remains to be seen.

HOST: So you're saying the market could go either down or up?

FIRST EXPERT: Don't put words in my mouth, Bob.

HOST: Mary?

SECOND EXPERT: I'm afraid I'm going to have to disagree with

John on this. I think what we're seeing here is a number of forces at work.

HOST: What forces would those be, Mary?

SECOND EXPERT: Dark forces, Bob. Powerful forces. Forces that threaten not just the city of Gondor, but the whole of Middle Earth.

HOST: But . . . isn't that the plot of *The Fellowship of the Rings*?

SECOND EXPERT: Whatever.

HOST: Norm? What's your take on the direction the market is going?

THIRD EXPERT: Reply hazy, Bob. Try again.

HOST: Are you reading from a Magic 8 Ball?

THIRD EXPERT (*putting something behind his back*): No.

HOST: All right, then! We're out of time, but our panel of insiders will be here again once again tomorrow night to offer their insights on whatever the market does tomorrow. So be sure to tune in! Or, you can just watch this show again.

THIRD EXPERT: Signs point to yes, Bob.

So, to summarize: Nobody really knows what the stock market is going to do. There may be some people who have some inside information about individual stocks, but they sure as hell are not going to go on television and tell *you*.

Does this mean that the stock market is really no more than a giant gambling casino? No! Gambling casinos are *much* more rational. The roulette wheel doesn't give a damn what's going on in the Middle East.

Don't get me wrong: I'm *not* saying you should take all your money out of the stock market and bet it on roulette. You get much better odds with blackjack.

13

HOW TO READ A CORPORATE ANNUAL REPORT

Mainly You Should Look at the Pictures

THE BEST WAY FOR YOU, the investor, to evaluate a corporation is to look at the corporation's annual report. This is an expensive, glossy, high-quality publication that the corporation puts out every year to reduce the likelihood that it will have any money left over to give to its stockholders.

There are four crucial elements of a standard corporation annual report:

- It should have a **formal photograph of the top corporate officers** posed in such a manner as to assure you, the investor, that the corporation is run by serious businesslike white men who, to judge from their facial expressions, have zucchinis up their butts.
- It should contain **random wads of corporate prose,** generated by a computerized corporate-prose generator,

explaining, in a manner that is vague and yet at the same time virtually incomprehensible, what an excellent year the corporation had thanks to the Vision and Leadership of its officers.

- It should have **photographs of impressive visual things—** molten steel molting, large robot machines doing things with their robot arms, cheerful workers working, industrial pipes going in all directions, etc.—to indicate that the corporation has been a very busy beaver, which is why it does not have time to stop and explain in any detail what it actually does.

- It should have **many charts, graphs, and columns of big numbers** designed to impress upon you, the investor, the fact that there are complicated financial things going on in the corporate world that you would never in a million years understand, so it's better if you leave these things to your corporate officers and go back to watching *American Idol.*

When all of these elements come together, you get a high-class annual report that should look something like this:

ANNUAL REPORT

WorldTechComTronic Gropemonger-Swingle Group, Inc.

"Lunging Forward Toward Tomorrow, Today"

The Fendelburg Plant
(shown before the unscheduled nuclear event)

Dear Shareholder:

We are pleased to report that we have had yet another banner year here at WorldTechComTronic Gropemonger-Swingle Group, Inc. But there is no need to take our word for it. Let's look at the hard factual numbers:

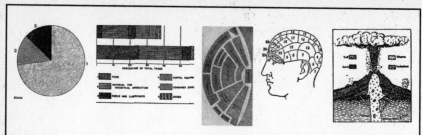

Note that, while our net fiduciary gross up-line downstream earnings were attenuated somewhat by the unscheduled nuclear event at the Fendelburg Plant, this was partially offset by a stronger-than-expected fourth-quarter incremental marginalized fiscal exuberation resulting from the relatively small number of survivors physically capable of filing lawsuits, thus yielding an overall adjusted "bottom line" numerical figure, allowing for the earth's rotation, of plus or minus 16.38 percent. Here are some more figures we would like to insert at this point:

HC									CVR/JKT	Coral
The Grace That Keeps This World				Editor:	SA				Insert	
Tom Bailey				Prod. Manager:	F Gregorio					
0307238016				Est. Prepared by:	F Gregorio					
10228794										
11-Oct	2005	Fall 2005		Estimate For:	Print					
$24.00										
6 1/8 x 9 1/4		Ink Colors	1/c	Jkt Specs:	4/c Matt Lam & Spot UV w/Foil & Embossing on 100 # c1s				Insert Specs	
288		Miscellaneous	-	# of colors	4	special inks	0	Bw Art		
Average		Rough Front	No	Upgrade Stock	100#C1S	backup colors	0	4c Art		
No		Case	3pc.	Upgrade Coating	Matte Film	Foil Background	Y	Printed		
0		Board	.068	Binders	2nd Coating	Gloss UV	Paperback w/flaps	N	Pages	
0		Endpapers	80# Colored	Foil		Y	Other	-	Stock	
-55	360 ppi	Manufacturing Location	Domestic	Emboss		Y			Bound As	

Manufacturing Plates & MR	Run	Initial Qty 1 15,000	Initial Qty 2 18,000	Initial Qty 3 20,000	Reprint Qty 1 5,000	Reprint Qty 2 7,500		Plant Initial	Reprint
$ 223.65	$ 489.60	$ 0.50	$ 0.50	$ 0.50	$ 0.53	$ 0.52	Text		
$ 268.92	$ -	$ 0.02	$ 0.01	$ 0.01	$ 0.05	$ 0.04	Comp (TXCO)	$ 3,456.00	
$ 336.95	$ 114.30	$ 0.14	$ 0.13	$ 0.13	$ 0.19	$ 0.17	Prfrd (TXPR)	$ 1,008.00	
$ 648.29	$ 624.43	$ 0.67	$ 0.66	$ 0.66	$ 0.78	$ 0.73	CE (TXCE)	$ 720.00	
front $ -	$ -	$ -	$ -	$ -	$ -	$ -	Design (TXDE)	$ 1,200.00	
ges $ -	$ -	$ -	$ -	$ -	$ -	$ -	Dummy (TXDE)		
s $ -	$ -	$ -	$ -	$ -	$ -	$ -	Scan 4c		

But as impressive as these numbers are, they do not tell the whole story. Because the heart of WorldTechComTronic Gropemonger-Swingle Group, Inc., is not statistics, but people—the dedicated workers who do the actual work over in Indonesia or someplace. They, truly, are our greatest resource, for without them, we would have to hire somebody else.

The People of WorldTechComTronic Gropemonger-Swingle

Yes, here at WorldTechComTronic Gropemonger-Swingle Group, Inc., we truly are a "family" in every sense of the word, except the sense of being related to or liking or caring about one another. And, as a family, we are engaged in many complicated and hard-to-understand fields of corporate endeavor in areas such as the following:

What We Are Doing at WorldTechComTronic Gropemonger-Swingle

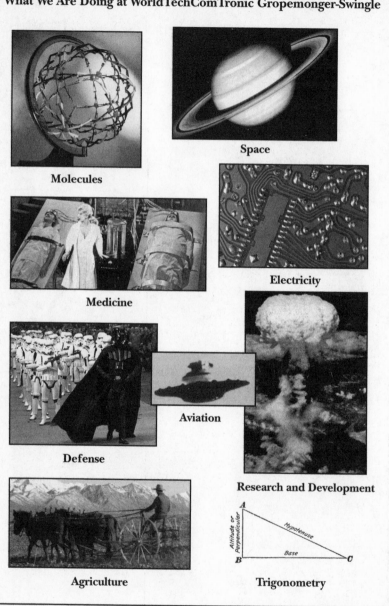

Molecules

Space

Medicine

Electricity

Defense

Aviation

Research and Development

Agriculture

Trigonometry

Yes, we have "a lot on our plate," but we truly believe that, with continued Vision and Leadership on our part, augmented by a third executive corporate jet that is currently on order, WorldTechComTronic Gropemonger-Swingle Group, Inc., is truly poised on the springboard of the cutting edge of innovation by thinking outside the box to advance boldly forward with all due caution from a position of strength toward the future. That is the pledge that we, your corporate officers, are proud to make to you in this Annual Report, which we would like to present to you, our shareholders, as a cherished gift in lieu of dividends.

God Bless You All,
Except for the Atheists,

L. Hobart Wackington
President, Chairman, and CEO
WorldTechComTronic Gropemonger-Swingle Group, Inc.

Your Board of Directors
Seated (*from left*): White man, white man, white man, white man, white man.
Standing (*from left*): White man, white man, white man, white man,
white man, woman. *Not shown:* Negro.

14

HOW TO MANAGE
A HEDGE FUND

Step One: Go to Lunch

ASK YOURSELF THIS QUESTION: Could you use an extra $200 million or more in income per year?

If your answer is "yes" or "I guess so," you should start a hedge fund. This is the hot new thing to do in the investment world. Remember in the late 1990s, when all those twenty-five-year-olds were starting dot-com businesses and getting rich on paper until the dot-com boom collapsed like a cheap lawn chair under a sumo wrestler and they all had to go back to boring, mediocre-paying, dead-end jobs like everybody else, and your heart was filled with joy?

Well, that's similar to the boom going on with hedge funds now. *Everybody* is starting them. Even as you read these words, there's a McDonald's employee somewhere saying, "I'm *tired* of asking four-year-olds which toy they want with their Happy Meal! I'm going to start a hedge fund!"

The reason hedge funds have become so popular is that there

is big money being made. HUGE money. Top hedge fund managers make *hundreds of millions of dollars a year.* These people don't vacation in Maui. These people leave Maui as a *tip.*

You need to get in on this. You don't want to be the last person in your car pool to start a hedge fund. So stop always letting "the other guy" start a hedge fund! Get off your butt and *start a hedge fund of your own.*

"But Dave," you object. "I don't know how to manage a hedge fund! I don't even know what a hedge fund is. I never even look at the newspaper business section unless for some reason it has a photo of Angelina Jolie."

No problem! I'm going to tell you everything you need to know in this chapter. I happen to be an expert in this field because I read an entire article about hedge funds in the *New York Times Magazine.* It took me nearly a half hour to finish the whole thing, and I had to read many big technical words such as "quantitative," "portfolio," "cognoscenti," "ferment," "whopping," and "Switzerland." But I did it. That is the kind of research that makes this book the kind of book that it is.

The first issue we need to address is: What, exactly, is a hedge fund? Basically, it is a large quantity, or "pool," of money, or "dough," usually billions of dollars, which you get from investors. You, the hedge fund manager, invest this money in various things, or "instruments," such as stocks, bonds, currencies, commodities, harmonicas, etc. If the fund makes a profit, you take a healthy percentage; if the fund loses money, you take a plane to Venezuela.

To be a good hedge fund manager, you can't base your investments on a hunch or whim. You must base them on research and hard data. Like, suppose you're at a restaurant with some people you know, and one of them, for the first time in your recollection, orders a bacon, lettuce, and tomato sandwich. And then another one says, "Hey, that sounds good! I'll have a BLT also!" And a third one goes, "What the heck! Me too!"

Now, to a normal person, this is nothing more than three people ordering the same sandwich. But you are not a normal person. You are a *hedge fund manager*, and you recognize that what you are seeing here could very well be a significant trend. Every day, hundreds of millions of people order sandwiches, and if even just, say, 5 percent of them suddenly order BLTs, the economic effect could be significant, as is shown by this simple formula:

$$B = LT^2$$

This tells us that there is going to be a major upsurge in the demand for bacon, which in turn means that bacon will be affected by the Law of Supply and Demand, as represented by this graph:

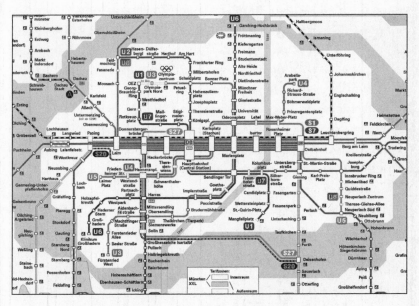

So now you know for a fact that the price of bacon will definitely go up, unless for some reason it goes down or remains the same. You *also* know that bacon actually comes from pigs, or, as they are known in the investment world, "porks."

Armed with this information, you call your commodities broker, and you purchase an option to buy, let's say, $1 billion worth of pork bellies. Then—this is very important—*you write this information down on a piece of paper,* so you will remember to sell this option before it expires. Otherwise, you're going to wake up one morning and find a UPS man at your door with like 517,000 tons of pig carcasses, and unless you have a really huge freezer, you are going to have to invite everybody you know to an emergency barbecue.

OK, now pay close attention, because here is where the "hedge" part of the hedge fund comes in. At this point, you have invested on the assumption that the price of pork will increase, which is called taking a "long position," or "going long," on pork. At least I'm pretty sure that's what it's called. It might be called "going short" on pork; I'm always getting those two confused. Just to be sure, ask another hedge fund manager which is which before you actually attempt this.

But whichever one it is, you need to "hedge" your bet on pork bellies by, at the same time, placing a financial bet *in the opposite direction.* How do you do that? You do it by asking yourself this question: If people are ordering *more* BLT sandwiches, what kind of sandwiches are they ordering *less* of?

Exactly: tuna. So at the same time you are going long (or short) for $1 billion in pork bellies, you want to go $1 billion *short* (or long) in tuna bellies. Then, having hedged your fund, you can go shopping for the helicopter-equipped yacht that you will be able to purchase with your share of the hedge fund profits.

That's it! That's all there is to running a hedge fund! The whole process should take you less than two hours per day, including lunch. And the beauty of it is, no matter what happens to the market, you are guaranteed to make huge amounts of money, according to the *New York Times Magazine,* which is solely responsible for the contents of this chapter.

I realize that you may have one or two lingering questions, such as: "Shouldn't I also take a strong position in mayonnaise?" and "How, exactly, do I get investors to give me $2 billion in the first place?" Those are good questions, and I wish I had time to answer them. But right now I really need a sandwich.

15

HOW TO GET RICH
IN REAL ESTATE

---

*Simple, Foolproof Techniques Unconditionally Guaranteed to
Work 100% of the Time for Anybody!*

Except You

I T'S EASY TO GET RICH IN REAL ESTATE. You don't have
to take any risk, or work hard, or even have a central nervous
system. That's how profitable real estate is!

How do we know this? The same way we know everything: television. Turn on your TV pretty much any weekend and click
through the channels, and soon you'll see an infomercial featur-
ing a real estate genius sitting poolside at a swank vacation resort
and explaining his simple system for getting rich, which he has
decided, out of generosity, to share with everybody in the world:

REAL ESTATE GUY: Hi! I'm Bob Pronghandle, and I'm sitting
poolside at this swank resort connoting success because I want

to tell you about my incredible program, Get Rich by Becoming Wealthy Making Big Money in Real Estate. You know, as I was driving here today in one of my several Rolls-Royces that I own because I have so much money from real estate, I was thinking about some amazing facts I'd like to share with you:

- Did you know that more millionaires got rich through real estate than any other way?
- Did you know that you can buy real estate without having any money?
- Did you know that over the long run, real estate always goes up in value?
- Did you know that every night, giant flying lobsters from Mars play Scrabble on top of the Chrysler Building?

Well, my incredible program, Get Rich by Becoming Wealthy Making Big Money in Real Estate, can show you how to *harness the power* of this information to break out of your loser infomercial-watching existence and achieve the lifestyle and Rolls-Royce quotient you have always dreamed of. But don't take my word for it! Joining me here poolside are two regular people like you, Norm and Gladys Hingler. Norm and Gladys, welcome!

NORM: Thanks, Bob. Good to be poolside.

REAL ESTATE GUY: Tell us about your experience with my incredible program, Get Rich by Becoming Wealthy Making Big Money in Real Estate.

NORM: Bob, in my own unrehearsed words, it is a dream come true. Our lives have totally changed. Like, last night, Gladys ate the whole jar of cashews from the minibar, and I took a look at the price and it was $12.50, and for a minute there I was like,

"ARE YOU OUT OF YOUR FRICKING *MIND,* GLADYS? TWELVE-FIFTY FOR LIKE SEVENTEEN FRICKING NUTS??" Then I remembered, "Hey! We're rich now, from real estate!" Although if you ask me, swank resort or not, $12.50 is a ripoff.

GLADYS: They weren't even that fresh.

NORM: It's OK to say "fricking," right? They told me don't say "fu . . ."

REAL ESTATE GUY (*interrupting*): OK, getting back to my program, Get Rich by Becoming Wealthy Making Big Money in Real Estate: Can you tell us how you found out about it?

NORM: Well, Bob, things were bad. I'd been working most of my life in the field of roadside fireworks sales, but it wasn't steady work.

GLADYS: It was two weeks a year.

NORM: So anyway, a year ago, two days before the Fourth of July, which is the height of our busy season, I had an on-the-job injury, which I won't go into the details of here.

GLADYS: He shot himself in the scrotum with a bottle rocket.

REAL ESTATE GUY: Huh. Well getting back to . . .

GLADYS: Is it OK to say "scrotum"?

NORM: It was a freak thing, Bob. It's a little demonstration I used to do where I launched the rocket from my pants. I called it the "Fart of Doom." It's a great sales booster—kids love it— and I did it a thousand times with no trouble, but this one time, I don't know what the hell happened—bad fuse, probably—but next thing I know I'm an unemployed man with a third-degree burn on the old nutsack that would *not* heal. Gladys was changing those bandages ten times a day. Is it OK that I said "fart?"

GLADYS: Do you have any idea how much pus a burned scrotum can produce?

REAL ESTATE GUY: No.

GLADYS: Most people don't.

NORM: So we were hurting for cash, I tell you. We have five children under the age of three, and it got to the point where we had to choose between buying food for them, or cigarettes. *No parent should have to make that choice, Bob.*

REAL ESTATE GUY: No.

NORM: So there we were: Our kids were starving, and our rent was past due. They even repossessed my Bowflex machine.

GLADYS: Like you ever used it.

NORM: It was the *humiliation*, goddammit, pardon my French.

REAL ESTATE GUY: So things were bad.

NORM: They were terrible. We didn't have two nickels to rub together. Gladys was thinking about turning tricks.

REAL ESTATE GUY: That's awful!

GLADYS: Not really, I saw something about it once on *The Maury Show*, "Hooker Housewives." You can make good money, set your own hours. And it's not like I was getting a lot of loving from Mister Scrotum Wound, here. He still can't get his . . .

REAL ESTATE GUY (*interrupting*): So you were desperate for money . . .

NORM: Right, we were desperate, and just when I thought we had hit bottom, we discovered a money-making concept that changed our lives.

REAL ESTATE GUY: My incredible program, Get Rich by Becoming Wealthy Making Big Money in Real Estate?

NORM: No, robbing convenience stores. Not with a gun, of course; we're both religious people. We had this fake bomb we made with duct tape.

GLADYS: Inside it was Tampax.

NORM: I'd say, "Give her the money, or I set off this bomb!" It worked the first two times, but the third time, the guy says,

"OK, OK! Here's your money!" But instead of cash, he pulls out a fricking *shotgun*. You can't trust anybody, Bob.

GLADYS: When Norm saw the shotgun, he jumped behind me and yelled, "Don't shoot me! It's *her* Tampax!"

NORM: I was thinking of the kids. They need a father.

REAL ESTATE GUY: So getting back to . . .

NORM: We ended up in prison, five to ten, and that's where I saw your infomercial, Bob.

REAL ESTATE GUY: You mean for my incredible program, Get Rich by Becoming Wealthy Making Big Money in Real Estate?

NORM: No, this was back when you were selling that kidney dialysis–by-mail program. Boy, *that* was a stinker, huh? I heard there were a *lot* of lawsu . . .

REAL ESTATE GUY: I don't think we need to . . .

NORM: But the thing was, I liked your style, Bob. First time I saw you, I said to Skag—Skag was my best friend in prison . . .

GLADYS: "Best friend," he calls it.

NORM (*ignoring her*): . . . I said, "Skag, this guy has something. When I watch his infomercial, I say to myself, now *that* is an infomercial."

REAL ESTATE GUY: Thank you.

NORM: So I started following your work, and when I made parole, first thing I did was get your tape, Get Rich by Getting Rich in whaddycallit.

REAL ESTATE GUY: Real estate.

NORM: Right. And Bob, in my own words, it is a dream come fricking true.

REAL ESTATE GUY: So you've made money?

NORM: Out the wazoo, Bob. If I can say "wazoo."

REAL ESTATE GUY: By applying the principles described in my program?

NORM: The what?

REAL ESTATE GUY: The principles of successful real estate investing.

NORM: Sure, whatever.

GLADYS: How come he made you get that tattoo, if he's your "best friend"?

NORM: Don't you make air quotes at me, bitch.

GLADYS: Oh, right, *I'm* the bitch.

REAL ESTATE GUY (*to camera*): There you have it: One couple's true story of how they achieved financial independence through my program, Get Rich . . .

NORM: At least I'm not a whore.

REAL ESTATE GUY: . . . by Becoming Wealthy . . .

GLADYS: Tell that to your "best friend," Skag.

REAL ESTATE GUY: . . . Making Big Money . . .

NORM (*lunging toward Gladys, knocking over the camera*): I SAID DON'T MAKE AIR QUOTES AT ME, BITCH!

VOICE OF REAL ESTATE GUY (*over sounds of struggle*): . . . in Real Estate!

VOICE OF GLADYS (*being choked*): WHORE!!

(THE SCREEN GOES DARK AS THE
CAMERA FALLS INTO THE POOL.)

I admit that the preceding is not a totally realistic depiction of a real estate infomercial. The real ones are even stupider. But the message is the same: *Anyone can make money in real estate!*

The only problem with this message is that it is, with all due respect, a tub of whale shit.[32] I say this because I personally have,

---

32. Pardon my French.

on numerous occasions, failed to make money in real estate. I've owned a string of houses, in good real estate markets and bad, and no matter what, I have almost always managed to not make money.

What's my secret? Simple: I make certain fundamental mistakes, and I make them consistently. These are proven, time-tested mistakes, and I believe that anybody—even somebody who has no previous experience losing money in real estate—can apply them.

Mistake Number One: Buy an Older House

The reason people usually give for buying an older house is that older houses have "character." What do we mean by "character"? We mean "dry rot."

The problem is that many, if not most, older houses were built in the past. Back then, people were stupider than they are today, and one result was that they built their houses largely out of wood. This was a mistake, because wood—and you can look this up if you don't believe me—comes from trees.

What's wrong with trees as a building material? Plenty. Go outside and examine a tree. From a distance, it appears to be a sturdy, permanent object, but when you examine it closely, you discover that it is a living organism, like a big hamster, except that virtually every part of the tree is constantly being eaten, bored into, nested on, or otherwise occupied by a vast teeming horde of ants, beetles, worms, termites, vines, toadstools, spiders, mosses, hornets, woodchucks, birds, chipmunks, squirrels, snakes, bats, and so on. A tree is nothing more than a giant hotel/buffet for critters. This is why the tree must keep committing acts of photosynthesis and growing new branches: If it didn't, in a matter of days it would be termite poop.

Cutting a tree down and calling it "lumber" does not change what it is: It's still a tree. Building a house out of "lumber" is really no different from building a house out of pepperoni or Cool Whip. *It's still edible.* Sooner or later, critters are going to resume eating it. The most deadly critter is the dry-rot fungus, an organism made up of tiny but voracious spores that, when magnified 127,000 times, look like this:

There are millions of these things munching away at the typical house. The older the house is, the more they've munched, until in time, what's holding the house up, structurally, is paint.

And that's not the only problem with the older house. It probably also has an antiquated electrical system, installed back in the days when electricity traveled at only 57 miles per hour and wires were fashioned from goat hair and beeswax. The plumbing system—consisting of pipes made from some material no longer considered safe, such as arsenic-coated lead—passes water about as smoothly as a ninety-one-year-old man with a prostate the size of a bowling ball. The windows, which cannot be opened, are as effective against drafts as a volleyball net. The heating system, although it has been modernized on several occasions (most recently 1928) was originally designed to burn some fuel that is no longer available, such as heretics. The air-conditioning system, if there is one, was apparently tacked onto the house in a single frenzied day by unskilled workers using only chainsaws. The current roof was put on during the administration of Warren G. Harding; the attic insulation consists primarily of spider corpses; and the basement is prone to flooding, as evidenced by the presence of a thriving coral reef.

In other words, an older home is a giant collection of costly defects held together by a few coats of grime and latex. But many people, when they look at an older home, don't see these problems: They see *character*. I know this because I am one of these people. More than once I have had my brain paralyzed by what psychiatrists call Old House Delusion Disease (OHDD).

My wife and I bought an old house that had every known old-house problem, including termites, not to mention a grand total of one closet, and *an entire room that had no electrical outlets*—a clear indication that the house was not built by or for people with a need for, say, lighting. Were we discouraged? No! We thought it was quaint!

Here's how delusional we were. We had plumbing problems (of course), and at one point, in an effort to fix a leak, some plumbing guys were crawling around under our house. They emerged holding some yellowed, crumbling, rolled-up newspapers, which they'd found wrapped around our pipes, apparently as insulation. We carefully unwrapped one of the newspapers and found that it was a *Miami Herald* from 1927. It had a story in it about Charles Lindbergh.

So consider our situation: There we were, confronted with stark evidence that our pipes, in addition to leaking, were very old. It's like being aboard a boat in the middle of the Pacific and discovering that not only were you sinking, but also that your hull was made entirely of Triscuits.

And how did we react to this horrible news? We were *thrilled*! Charles Lindbergh! It was so *charming*!

The plumbers were also very excited, but in their case it was because they knew we would be putting all their children through Harvard.

Old House Delusion Disease is very powerful. Usually, when

you buy an old house, you hire professional house inspectors. These inspectors are very thorough: They spend a whole day crawling around the house, and then they give you a detailed, written report, which says *DO NOT BUY THIS HOUSE, YOU IDIOT.*

Not in so many words, of course. The report breaks the house down by major defects, which are further broken down into sub-defects, sometimes hundreds of them. The house, according to this report, consists entirely of defects. You *read* this report, but because you have OHDD, none of it actually penetrates into your brain. Your brain remains impervious, even when the inspector goes out of his way to warn you about serious problems:

INSPECTOR: OK, there's something I want to show you here in the living room . . .

YOU: Don't you *love* the living room? It has such character! The molding!

INSPECTOR: Right, about the molding, I wanted you to see this. *(The inspector takes a screwdriver and taps the tip gently against the molding. The molding disappears in a smokelike puff of wood parti-cles, and then a large part of the wall itself collapses, leaving a gaping hole, through which can be seen, in the gloom, an exposed wire that periodically emits a shower of sparks, illuminating a dripping pipe covered with green slime. A rat darts past, pursued by what appears to be a boa constrictor.)*

YOU: Ha ha! These quirky old houses! That can be repaired, right?

INSPECTOR: Well, yes, I suppose it could, if you're willing to completely . . .

YOU: I'm not worried about cosmetic problems, as long as the house is structurally sound. They knew how to build these babies in the old days. *(You stamp your foot on the floor to empha-size this point. Your foot goes through the floor.)*

INSPECTOR: Um, that's another thing I wanted to mention. Your floor joists have been almost entirely eaten away.

YOU *(retracting your foot)*: Termites? No biggie! A lot of these old houses have termites! We can just have it treated by . . .

INSPECTOR: Actually, it's beavers.

YOU: Beavers?

INSPECTOR: They're building a dam in the basement.

YOU:

INSPECTOR: I've never seen that before.

YOU *(recovering)*: The kids have been wanting a pet!

At this point the inspector, who has dealt with OHDD before, gives up and edges out of the room, taking care not to put too much weight on any one part of the floor.

You, of course, go ahead and buy the house. As a true OHDD victim, you would buy this house if it was actively on fire. Once it is yours, you begin calling what will become a never-ending parade of skilled, highly paid craftsmen, who will spend so much time at your house that eventually they will become a part of your family and invite you to attend all their children's graduations from Harvard.

To summarize what we have covered so far, the first proven technique guaranteed to lose you money in real estate is to buy an older house. This leads us to:

Mistake Number Two: Buy a New House

Unlike old houses, which fall apart over time, new houses start falling apart immediately. Often the last subcontractors on the job have to sprint from the house as it begins to collapse around them, like Indiana Jones in the Temple of Doom.

There are several reasons for this. First, new houses are crap. No, wait, that's unfair to crap. In parts of rural Nepal, people make houses out of actual dung, and these houses are much sturdier than new American homes in subdivisions with names like Manor Oaks Estates Phase IV.

One problem is materials. We've established that a major flaw in older-home construction was that the houses were built out of wood, a material that not only rots and burns but also is viewed as lunch by large segments of the animal and fungus kingdoms. So today, new houses are built out of: wood.

Yes! We've learned nothing! Only now, thanks to modern manufacturing techniques, the wood we use is much flimsier. Take the "two-by-four." This was originally a sturdy piece of lumber that measured two inches by four inches, which is how it got its name.[33] But over the years, the lumber industry—whose executives live in homes constructed entirely of stainless steel—has been cutting costs by reducing lumber sizes, so that now a "two-by-four" is more along the lines of a Popsicle stick:

Modern "Two-by-Four"

(actual size)

Scientists in the lumber industry are working day and night to reduce the size of the "two-by-fours" even more. They dream of a

---

33. Its name is Harold.

day, in the not-so-distant future, when a "two-by-four" will be invisible to the naked human eye, and a single termite will be able to consume an entire home in forty-five minutes.

Another problem with new homes is the quality of the builders. Don't get me wrong: I'm not saying there are no good builders. There *are* good builders: Their names are Arnold and Herb Frinker, and they are honest, competent, reliable, and reasonably priced. They retired in 1987.

But the rest of the field is pretty bleak. In parts of the nation, all you need to do to become a professional house builder is take a brief course and pass an exam that is not overly demanding, as we see from these actual questions:

Professional House-Builder License Exam Questions

1. **What type of vehicle should a professional house builder drive?**

   a. A truck type of vehicle.

   (Correct Answer: a.)

2. **You're building a house for a customer who is locked into a very rigid move-in date. You have repeatedly assured this customer that the house will absolutely, positively, definitely, no question, count on it 110 percent, be finished in six months. Assume that the date is March 1. When will this house be finished?**

   a. You mean, like, *completely* finished?

   b. Not this year, that's for sure.

   c. How the hell should I know?

   (Correct Answer: These are all correct.)

3. **A buyer has just moved into a house you built and is calling you repeatedly to complain that there is a toilet installed in the middle of the living room; that there is no floor in the kitchen; and that hot water is gushing from the electrical outlets. How do you respond to these problems?**
   a. Get a new phone number.
   b. Explain that these are normal things caused by the house "settling."
   c. What problems?
   (Correct Answer: There is nothing wrong with any of these answers.)

To review what we have learned about real estate so far: It is a huge mistake to buy an older house, because it will fall apart and you will forever be repairing it. The same is true if you buy a new house. But you can't buy *any* kind of house unless you have money, which leads us to:

Mistake Number Three: Get a Mortgage

A mortgage is a great big wad of money that you borrow so you can buy a house that you cannot, by any sane standard, afford.

There are many different kinds of mortgages available, including fixed rate 30-year, fixed rate 15-year, variable rate 30-year, variable rate 10-year jumbo with balloon, variable fixed year 15-balloon jumbo rate, and 30 variably rated ballooning yearly jumbos, to name just a few.

Before applying for a mortgage, you should thoroughly familiarize yourself with the advantages and disadvantages of each type of mortgage. Then you should pick one at random, because they all work exactly the same way: Every month, you send a payment to your lender, and no matter how many times you do this, *you still owe the same total amount.* It's like the movie *Groundhog Day,* where no matter what Bill Murray did, he always ended up starting over in exactly the same place.

Fact: Inside the mortgage business, customers are commonly referred to as "Bill Murrays."

The difference is that *Groundhog Day* eventually ends, whereas a mortgage never does. To date, the Egyptians have made more than 55,000 monthly mortgage payments on the pyramids, and they still owe exactly as much on their mortgage—a 30-year variable jumbo balloon—as they did in 2600 B.C. (They're thinking about refinancing.) You should just accept the fact that you're going to have a giant mortgage balance until you die, possibly as a result of beaver bites.

Conclusion

As we have seen, real estate is an exciting field, offering many opportunities for a financial novice such as yourself to screw up. In this chapter, I have done my best to cover as much ground as possible without imparting a single shred of useful information. Now it's up to you to get out there and apply these techniques. Because as the late football coach Vince "Vince" Lombardi so often said: "If you don't get up off the bench and get into the game, you can never suffer a career-ending knee injury." Those words are still very true today, and although Coach Lombardi has passed away, I have no doubt whatsoever that somehow, somewhere, his mortgage lives on.

16

HOW TO NEGOTIATE
A "WIN-WIN" OUTCOME

You Must Crush Your Opponent Like an Insect

L ET'S SAY TWO MEN—call them Bob and John[34]—both want to buy a new car. They go to the same dealership on the same day and order the same model of car, with exactly the same options. Yet John pays $3,500 less for the car than Bob does. Why?

Simple. Throughout the entire course of his discussions with the car salesman, John was holding an eighteen-inch machete. This basic tactic—which rarely occurs to most car buyers—gave John a big edge in his negotiations, an edge that he was able to take to the bank.[35]

Yes, knowing how to negotiate is a very useful skill—and not just in financial transactions. Although you may not realize it, you're negotiating constantly, from when you wake up in the morning and negotiate with your spouse for access to the bath-

---

34. These are a different "Bob" and "John" from the "Bob" and "John" in the Introduction.
35. When he got to the bank, he was able to withdraw $15,000 in cash, even though he did not have an account.

room; to when you negotiate with your kids to get them to stop playing their video game, "Death Killer of Fatal Murdering II: The Slaying" for *ten freaking minutes;* to when you negotiate with your boss to give you a raise and a promotion, or at least a better chair; to when you go to bed at night and negotiate with your spouse over whether you're going to have any kind of intimate carnal relations at all during the current fiscal year.

So if you want to get ahead in life and the bathroom, you need to know the rules of effective negotiating. The most important one is: *Never pay list price.* I mean *never.* For *anything,* including intimate carnal relations with your spouse.[36] List price is for *suckers.* If somebody tries to charge you list price, you need to make it clear to this person that you are a savvy individual who knows how the game is played, and you need to *stick to your guns:*

You: How much is it?

Person: $1.50.

You: That's too much.

Person: What?

You: It's too much. I'll give you 75 cents.

Person: This is a *toll booth.* The toll is $1.50.

You: Eighty cents. But that's the best I can do.

Person: But *everybody* pays $1.50.

You: That's your *retail* price. *You* didn't pay that much. Listen, I understand you need to make a profit. But let's work together here. Let's find a middle ground we can both be happy with.

Police officer: What seems to be the problem here?

Person: He doesn't want to pay the toll.

---

36. Just so you know: Your spouse usually charges $50.

Police officer: You have to pay the toll.

You: I realize that, Officer, and I am perfectly willing to pay a reasonable price. We're negotiating that right now.

Police officer: OK, I'm going to give you a ticket for obstructing traffic. You just got yourself a $250 fine.

You: I'll give you $125. Take it or leave it.

Police officer: Is that a machete?

See how easy it is? By sticking to your guns and insisting on a better price, you have negotiated yourself into a position where, instead of settling for the same deal that "everybody" gets, you will receive special treatment.

Most of us experience our first serious financial negotiations when we attempt to buy a car. A lot of people hate buying cars, because they feel that car dealerships use unethical sales tactics. This is not true! Car dealerships operate under an extremely strict code of ethics. Here it is:

Car Dealership Code of Ethics

- **ETHIC 1.** The salesperson shall never, under any circumstances, reveal the True Price of the car to the customer *until after the customer has agreed to purchase the car.* Until that point, the True Price shall be shrouded in deep mystery. Even though the dealership is in the business of selling cars, and has been selling cars for years, and sells cars every single day, including the exact car that the customer is looking at; and even though the dealership knows to the exact penny how much the car costs, and how much profit the dealership needs to make, the salesperson will insist that he has NO IDEA what the True

Price is. The only way he can find out the True Price is to ask the Manager, and he cannot ask the Manager until *after the customer has agreed to purchase the car.*

- **ETHIC 2.** Once the customer has agreed to purchase the car, the customer and the salesperson shall work out an Offer. The salesperson shall then inform the customer that it is the lowest Offer that he, the salesperson, has ever dared to take to the Manager, and that he could very well be in physical danger. But, darn it, the salesperson *really likes* the customer, so he is going to give it a shot.

- **ETHIC 3.** The salesperson will then leave the customer alone sitting on a hard plastic chair in the little sales cubicle for a period of time that is not less than the gestation period of a yak. During this time the customer shall have nothing to do except stare at the framed photographs of the salesperson's children, who shall look cute but waiflike and hungry.

- **ETHIC 4.** If the salesperson has no children of his own, he may use photographs of waifs cut out of *National Geographic.*

- **ETHIC 5.** When the salesperson returns, he shall look weary but triumphant. He shall inform the customer that the Manager was very, very angry about getting such a low Offer and at one point struck the salesperson with a telephone directory. But the salesperson fought for the customer like a tiger and was able to get the Manager to agree to a price that, while somewhat higher than the Offer, is still so low that the dealership is actually *losing money* on the deal, PLUS the deal *includes floor mats,* which, according to the salesperson, are worth, like, $17,000, making this deal so amazing that the dealership will probably go out of business at any moment because of its insane generosity, so the customer had better sign the deal *right now.*

- **ETHIC 6.** If the customer balks, steps 2 through 5 shall be repeated as often as necessary, until the customer has been in the sales cubicle so long that his butt has become chemically bonded to the plastic chair and the salesperson is returning from the Manager's office with blood on his shirt from fighting so hard against the Manager and getting a price so low that he, the salesperson, will not make any commission at all, and his children will have nothing to eat except boiled gravel, but that is all right, because the salesperson has formed a deep personal bond with the customer and cares only about getting him this excellent deal. Finally the customer, realizing that he is in danger of spending his golden years in this cubicle, will break down and agree to the deal. The customer now believes that his ordeal is finally over, and that he at last knows the True Price.

- **ETHIC 7.** The customer is an idiot.

- **ETHIC 8.** At this point the salesperson shall broach the issue of "undercoating." The salesperson shall explain that, although the manufacturer did a thorough job of finishing the *upper* part of the car—the frame, body, interior, engine, transmission, etc.—for some mysterious, totally inexplicable reason, the manufacturer failed to protect the *underside* of the car, which, the way the salesperson describes it, is made of low-grade shirt cardboard, so that, if left uncoated, it could dissolve at any moment and dump the customer and his loved ones onto the interstate at speeds in excess of 70 miles per hour, and, as a fellow parent with waifs of his own, the salesperson simply cannot sit idly by and allow that to happen to a customer he cares so deeply about.

• **ETHIC 9.** Once the customer has agreed to purchase the undercoating—and the customer *will* agree to purchase the undercoating—the salesperson shall broach various other essential dealer-installed features that the manufacturer, incredibly, forgot to include with the car, including: an alarm system that will annoy the hell out of everybody within a two-mile radius but never actually summon help; an Extended Total Customer Security Protection Plan offering numerous benefits that the customer will never actually benefit from; embossed-leather owner's manual; driver's-side ashtray light; lug nut defroster; moth deflector; rear-seat catheters, etc. In time the customer, weak from lack of food and realizing that the best years of his life are slipping away, will agree to purchase all of these things.

• **ETHIC 10.** But the customer shall *still* not know the True Price, not until it is finally time for the Ritual Signing of the Papers. This is when the customer discovers that, in addition to the price of the car and all the extras and the taxes and the license and registration fees, he has to pay for "dealer prep." Dealer prep means cleaning the shmutz off the car, removing the stickers, adding fluids, etc., so that the car can actually be driven. In other words, the dealership, after charging the customer many thousands of dollars for the car and the various extras, is now going to charge the customer several hundred MORE dollars *for getting the car into usable condition.* This is not unlike a restaurant that lists steak on the menu for $23, and then, when a diner orders the steak, the restaurant charges $5 more for "thawing and cooking." But the customer, like millions of car buyers before him, will pay the "dealer prep," because by this point, after hours of intense cubicle pressure, the customer has the functional intelligence of a Rice Krispie.

As we see, when you enter a car dealership, you are going to be exposed to a very tough ethics code. Few people can stand up against it. I, for one, cannot. I'm the world's worst car buyer. I come from a long line of Presbyterians, who get their name from the Greek words *pre,* meaning "people," and *sbyterian,* meaning "who always pay retail."

In ancient times Presbyterians were nomadic goat traders. They would arrive at a market with, say, fifty goats, and then, after several hours of bargaining, they would leave with twenty-three goats. Everybody loved to do business with the Presbyterians. The reason they became nomadic in the first place was that they traded their entire village for a pound of lentils.

So when I'm in a car dealership, I am basically prey. My idea of an opening tactical salvo is to look at the car's sticker price and say to the salesperson, "This looks like a good deal! Are you sure you're making enough profit on this?" I buy *all* the dealer add-ons. I buy Extended Total Customer Security Protection Plans for *other customers.*

If you're like me, you should never go into a car dealership, or even *walk past* a car dealership, alone. You should always take along a designated negotiator. I recommend my friend Gene Weingarten. He actually *likes* to bargain with car salespersons. It's a blood sport for him. He can sit in the cubicle for *days* and not change his position by a dime. He would rather undergo a vasectomy with a WeedEater than purchase undercoating.

Consider the Louisiana Purchase. In 1803, President Thomas Jefferson negotiated a deal with France under which the United States agreed to pay $15 million, in return for which France gave the U.S. full title to 800,000 square miles, or nearly 525 million acres, which works out to *3 cents per acre*. Thus, in one stroke, Jefferson doubled the size of the fledgling nation and gave it control over a vast territory, strategically vital and rich in natural resources, stretching all the way from the Mississippi River to the Rocky Mountains:

The Louisiana Purchase
As Thomas Jefferson Negotiated It

Gene would have gotten a *much* better deal. He would have started by demanding that France knock at least $2 million off the asking price because the package included North Dakota. Gene's position would have been that he was doing the French a *favor,* taking North Dakota off their hands. He would have also demanded that France knock off another $3 million because the Great Plains were basically covered with bison dung.

In addition to demanding a lower price, Gene would have insisted that France sweeten the deal by throwing in various extras. Ultimately France would give in, just to get rid of Gene, and the Louisiana Purchase would have been more along these lines:[37]

The Louisiana Purchase
If Gene Weingarten Had Negotiated It

Which brings us to real estate. Negotiating to buy or sell a house is different from negotiating for a car, because—to name just one factor—most cars do not have bathrooms. Also, your negotiating opponent, instead of being a professional car salesperson armed with a powerful set of ethics capable of reducing

---

37. When I wrote this chapter, I told Gene what I was going to say about him and the Louisiana Purchase, and he agreed completely. He also said this: "Actually, the biggest idiocy was the purchase of Manhattan. We gave up WAY more trinkets than we had to."

you to a whimpering blob of drooling stupidity, is a regular human just like you. But that is no excuse for decency. There is *never* room for decency in negotiations.

In negotiating for a house, the first thing you need to know is whether you are the buyer or the seller. To determine which one you are, look in your yard. Is there a FOR SALE sign? If so, you are probably the seller. If you don't have a yard, you are probably the buyer.

Now pay close attention here, because we are coming to the meat of real estate negotiations: If you are the *seller*, you want to get the *highest* possible price, which you obtain by presenting the house as a highly desirable property; whereas if you are the *buyer*, you want to pay the *lowest* possible price, which you obtain by suggesting that the house is basically a big house-shaped wad of bison dung. Be sure that, in the heat of negotiations, you do not become confused:

YOU: I'm sorry, but this house is basically a big house-shaped wad of bison dung.

YOUR OPPONENT: Wait a minute. Aren't you the seller?

YOU: Ohmigod, you're right! I mean it's a highly desirable property. Sorry!

YOUR OPPONENT: Don't apologize! I do that all the time.

Because real estate negotiations are so confusing, you may want to use the services of a real estate broker. This is a highly trained professional who, in exchange for receiving a commission, relieves you of all the worry and headache of figuring out what you would do with the extra money if you weren't paying a commission.

The best way to choose a real estate broker is by the quality of the broker's photograph in the newspaper classified ads. I'm not sure when this happened, but at some point, real estate brokers, at least where I live in South Florida, started running *serious* glamour photos of themselves. The result is that, in many real estate classifieds, you can't tell for sure what's being advertised:

Thelma Skellnacker

REAL ESTATE BROKER
THELMA SKELLNACKER
PRESENTS

**5-BEDROOM 4-BATH COLONIAL
RECENTLY RENOVATED KITCHEN
BEAUTIFUL WOODED LOT
WHISPERING MUSHROOM ESTATES
EXCELLENT SCHOOLS**

← Take a gander at *those* garbonzos!

House

But enough about real estate. This isn't even supposed to be the real estate chapter. This is the chapter on negotiating, and it is time to sum up what you have learned:

1. Negotiating is very important.
2. Thomas Jefferson was an idiot.
3. Never pass up an opportunity to trade goats with a Presbyterian.
4. You should NOT pay for the undercoating. You should never pay for ANYTHING that you don't really need.
5. This book, for example, was a *horrible* investment.

17

INCOME TAXES: BUILDING BLOCKS OF OUR GREAT NATION AND LIFEBLOOD OF OUR SACRED DEMOCRATIC WAY OF LIFE

How to Avoid Paying Them

AS THE OLD SAYING GOES, "Nothing in life is certain except death and taxes. Also, O.J. was guilty."

How true these words are. If our government is going to be able to provide for the common good, everybody has to contribute his or her fair share in the form of taxes. And when I say "everybody," I mean, "not everybody." Because the truth is that a lot of people don't pay taxes. Poor people, for example. Also many rich people. Also a fair number of middle-income people.

In fact, when you get right down to it, there is a great big old wad of people who don't pay taxes. Our goal, in this chapter, is to show you how to become a member of that wad, without winding up in federal prison giving mandatory backrubs to a cellmate known as "Ramrod."

The trick is to understand the U.S. Tax Code. This is a collection of laws passed by the United States Congress, a legislative body composed of people you hated in high school. Since Congress is responsible for the content of the tax laws, if you ever have a question about your taxes, all you have to do is ask your congressperson, and he or she will be happy to give you a simple, clear, and definite answer.

That was of course a joke. Congress has *no idea* what's in the U.S. Tax Code. Members of Congress don't read the laws they pass, because this would take valuable time away from their congressional duties, such as drinking coffee with people who will give them money so they can get reelected to Congress and continue to carry out their duties.

But let's not be too harsh on Congress. The truth is that *nobody* understands the U.S. Tax Code. It's far too difficult even for really smart people. Back in 1955, Albert Einstein, acting on a dare from some fellow geniuses at a genius party, attempted to read the Tax Code, and within minutes he keeled over dead. "His brain looked like tapioca," the coroner said.

Actual Photographs Showing Effects of
Reading Tax Code on Albert Einstein's Brain

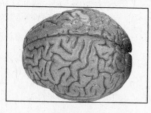

Before

After

SOURCE: Dan Rather

And that was fifty years ago, when the Tax Code was only a few million words. It's *much* bigger now—so big that nobody dares to go near it. It's kept in a locked, windowless vault in the basement of the Internal Revenue Service building. Every day at 3 p.m. a taxpayer is selected at random, audited, then thrown into this vault. There's usually a scream, followed by silence, followed by a massive burp. The next day the Tax Code is bigger.

But it's not just big. It's also really, really hard to understand. Pick any random sentence from the Tax Code, and it will look something like this:

> Biannually adjusted negative graduated monetary yields benefiting ordinary net gross optimization must accrue monthly aggregates.

You have no idea what that means, right? And yet this is a short and fairly clear sentence by Tax Code standards. Most of it is much worse, which means ordinary humans like you have no chance of understanding it. And the reason for this is simple: You're not *supposed* to understand it. It's designed specifically to *prevent* you from understanding it. That's right: The truth is that *the U.S. Tax Code is written entirely in code.* Hence the name "Tax Code."

It's filled with secret messages that only certain people are supposed to understand. For example, the sentence printed above was inserted into the Tax Code in 1957 by a Georgia congressman named Henry Hornbucket solely to send a secret message to a secretary with whom he was having an affair. To decode Rep. Hornbucket's message, read only the first letter of each word:

> Biannually adjusted negative graduated monetary yields benefiting ordinary net gross optimization must accrue monthly aggregates.

That's right: The entire purpose of this sentence—a sentence that, over the decades, has resulted in countless hours of taxpayer anguish, millions of dollars in accounting fees, and numerous bitter, drawn-out legal battles, and ultimately required a ruling by the U.S. Supreme Court—was so that a now-deceased politician could tell his girlfriend, "BANG MY BONGO, MAMA."

The Tax Code is riddled with such secret messages. The entire purpose of the so-called "Tax Reform Act of 1997"—a document of more than 1,600 pages—was to enable a group of congressional interns to announce a keg party.

But secret personal messages are only one reason why the Tax Code is so huge and confusing. Another one is "loopholes," which are special provisions that congresspersons stick in there to give special tax breaks to certain people. These loopholes are very hard for ordinary taxpayers to spot. For example, take a look at this section of the Tax Code:

SEC. 249. LIMITATION ON DEDUCTION OF BOND PREMIUM ON REPURCHASE

Subchapt. B, Part VIII, Sec. 249

Mr. Robert Fringleman of 37 Twitching Sphincter Lane, Greenwich, Connecticut, shall not have to pay any federal taxes at all, ever. Bob, thanks for the large campaign contribution! Please let me know if I can be of any further service to you or Muriel. Love always, your obedient servant U.S. Rep. Darrell P. Longfluke.

No deduction shall be allowed to the issuing corporation for any premium paid or incurred upon the repurchase of a bond, debenture, note, or certificate or other evidence of indebtedness which is convertible into the stock of the issuing corporation, or a corporation in control of, or controlled by, the issuing corporation, to the extent the repurchase price exceeds an amount equal to the adjusted issue price plus a normal call premium on bonds or other evidences of indebtedness which are not convertible.

Once again, we have a glob of prose that makes no sense to you, a regular human. In fact, this section is specifically designed to cause you to fall asleep by the word "debenture." That way, you are highly unlikely to notice the loophole. And where, exactly, *is* the loophole? OK, do you see the "line" under the words "*Subchapt. B, Part VIII*, Sec. 249"? That's not a line: *That's the loophole.* It's written in tiny one-point type, which is known in Washington as the "tax loophole font." When we magnify that little line ten times, here's what we see:

> Mr. Robert Fringleman of 17 Twitching Sphincter Lane, Greenwich, Connecticut, shall not have to pay any federal taxes at all, ever. Bob, thanks for the large campaign contribution! Please let me know if I can be of any further service to you or Marcia! Love always, your obedient servant U.S. Rep. Darnell P. Lungfluke.

The Tax Code contains *thousands* of these loopholes, each one giving a generous tax break to some plugged-in individual or corporation. It goes without saying that none of these loopholes applies to regular dirtbag taxpayers such as you.

So what can you do to reduce your tax burden? The best way is to keep accurate financial records and thoroughly familiarize yourself with the applicable tax laws, so you can avail yourself of every legal advantage. Like you would ever do *that*. This leaves you with Option B: cheating.

The trick to successful tax cheating, according to the American Society of Crooked Tax Accountants of America, is "Don't be a moron." You don't want to do anything in your tax return that will raise a "red flag" and target you for an audit. Some common mistakes are:

- Using a suspicious-sounding nickname on your tax return, such as "Icepick Willy," "Johnny Two Knuckles," or "Martha Stewart."

- Writing "YOU'LL NEVER CATCH ME, IRS CUBICLE-DWELLING SLUGS!" in large red letters across the front of your 1040 form.[38]
- Claiming an absurd refund amount, such as "eleven zillion dollars."[39]

But if you use common sense and cheat in a responsible manner, you have no reason to be concerned. To quote Internal Revenue Service Commissioner Harmon Sneegart: "The odds are really good that we'll never catch you. How the hell can we? We're federal employees! We take two hundred fifty-three days off a year!"

So let's take a look at the standard Form 1040 and see where you should focus your tax-cutting efforts:

Taxpayer name: Here's a tax-saving opportunity few taxpayers take advantage of: Instead of simply writing your name, write your name plus the word "DECEASED." This can save you big money down the road. In case the IRS checks up on you, you should also change your telephone answering-machine message to something like, "Hi, this is [*your name*]. I can't come to the phone right now because I am currently dead, at least for tax purposes."

Presidential Election Campaign Fund checkoff box: If you check this box, $3 of your taxes will be earmarked for a special fund to pay for presidential campaigns. Notice that the government does *not* permit you to earmark money for poor people, or sick people, or national defense. No, the govern-

---

38. IRS regulations require blue or black ink for statements of this nature.
39. Always use a nonrounded number such as "one zillion dollars and 63 cents."

ment permits you to earmark money only for the purpose of enabling politicians to produce TV commercials designed to appeal to voters who have the IQ of a Vienna sausage. To make matters worse, some of this federal campaign money goes to candidates who have about as much chance of getting elected president as SpongeBob SquarePants. In 2004, for example, more than $800,000 of earmarked U.S. taxpayer dollars went to Lyndon LaRouche, a convicted felon and complete space loon who has been running for president since 1980, and who has claimed, among other things, that Walter Mondale was a Soviet agent and Queen Elizabeth II is a drug dealer.[40] If you check the Presidential Election Campaign Fund box, it won't affect the amount of tax you owe, but I will lose all respect for you.

Filing status: Your choices here are Single, Married, Married but Messing Around, Head of Household, Foot of Household, Native American, Presbyterian Filing Jointly, Groin of Household, Biped, and None of the Above. I don't care which one you check. I'm still pissed off about Lyndon LaRouche.

Exemptions: This is where you tell the IRS how many dependents you have. In calculating your dependents, you should bear two things in mind:

1. The more dependents you have, the less tax you owe.

2. Nowhere in the U.S. Tax Code does it explicitly state, in so many words, that these dependents cannot be imaginary, if you are catching my drift.

Income: From a tax standpoint, income is the exact opposite of exemptions: The less you have, the better. Smart rich people have understood this for years. For example, on his 2003 tax re-

---

40. She is, of course. But still.

turn, Bill Gates reported a total income of $6,437.62. This was so low that even the IRS became suspicious, but when auditors attempted to examine Mr. Gates's records, the entire U.S. government computer system (which uses the Microsoft Windows operating system) went berserk—erasing data, generating porn e-mails, launching nuclear missiles at Belgium, etc. Within minutes a high-level federal decision was made not to challenge Mr. Gates on his income, nor his 8,257 children.[41]

Business expenses: Legitimate business expenses are tax deductible. How do we define the term "legitimate business expense"? We define it—and bear in mind, we are words in a published book—as "pretty much everything." Be aware, however, that if you claim a large amount of business deductions, the IRS may send an agent around to check you out, and if your business does not, in a strictly technical sense, exist, it's a good idea to be prepared:

IRS AGENT: So you're claiming that last year, you had business expenses totaling $78,473.52 to operate a commercial snail farm?

YOU: That's correct. I have over 37,000 head of commercial snail. The veterinary bills alone are *ridiculous.*

IRS AGENT: May I see this farm?

YOU: Certainly. It's right here in the backya . . . Oh my GOD! The gate is open! They *ESCAPED!*

Of course there's always the chance that, even if you cheat in a responsible manner, you'll be called in for a tax audit. This is not the "end of the world." Remember that, as a taxpayer, you have

---

41. All named Ashley.

certain rights. For example, the auditor cannot use a cattle-prod setting greater than 5,000 volts.

So if you're called in for an audit, the important thing is: *Don't panic.* Gather up all your financial records, consult with your lawyer and your accountant, and then, on the appointed day, flee to Uzbekistan. If you get caught, remember: *You never heard of this book.*

18

GET RICH THE
DONALD TRUMP WAY!

Whatever the Hell That Is

WHEN YOU TALK ABOUT MONEY, sooner or later the name Donald Trump comes up. Here's an individual who has it all—a huge fortune, a vast real estate empire, a hit "reality" TV show, and a bevy of vivacious, beautiful former wives. So if you're interested in achieving wealth and success of your own, your obvious question is: What's the deal with his hair?

Nobody really knows. One thing is certain: His hair color is not normally found on humans. Where it *is* found is on troll dolls, and on certain snack foods, as exemplified by the World's Largest Cheeto (currently on display in a bar in Algona, Iowa).

From left: Donald Trump; troll doll; World's Largest Cheeto

There's also some question about exactly where on Mr. Trump's body his hair originates. It appears, from the unnatural way it swoops around, to be coming from somewhere below his neck, or possibly from an entirely different person. Mr. Trump is usually surrounded by staff people; there's a theory that one of these people is actually employed as a comb-over donor, whose hair passes down through his pants leg, across to Mr. Trump's pants leg, and then up the back of Mr. Trump's body to Mr. Trump's head.

But the point of this chapter is not that, despite being a well-known billionaire who presumably has access to mirrors, Mr. Trump goes around looking like a vaguely alien life-form. The point of this chapter is to answer the question: How did Mr. Trump get so rich, and can you do the same thing, while maintaining a normal appearance?

Well, you are in luck, because Mr. Trump has written a book of advice. It's entitled: *My Name Is Not Important.*

Ha ha! I am just kidding. It goes without saying that Mr. Trump's book, like everything else associated with Mr. Trump and Mr. Trump's empire, prominently features Mr. Trump's name ("Trump"). The official title of his book is:

TRUMP
How to Get Rich
Big Deals from the Star of *The Apprentice*

The bad news is, this book is more than 240 pages long. The good news is, a lot of these pages are either blank or nearly blank, plus there are a lot of pictures, many of them of Donald Trump. Most of the book consists of very short chapters with titles like "Maintain Your Momentum," often illustrated by anecdotes from Donald Trump's own personal life. In one of the chapters, Mr. Trump deals directly and courageously with the issue of his hair.

I read the entire book, which took me almost one hour. If you don't have that kind of time, but you would still like to get rich the Donald Trump way, you can simply read the bullet points below, which I believe summarize all of the key information contained in the book. If you don't even have time to read that much, you can go directly to the parts about the hair, which are indicated by Cheetos instead of bullet points.

KEY POINTS IN DONALD TRUMP'S BOOK *HOW TO GET RICH*

- Money isn't everything.
- But just for the record, Donald Trump is a major billionaire.
- You need to hire good people. Good people are better to hire than bad people.
- Stay focused! For a while in the late eighties, Donald Trump flew off to Europe to attend fashion shows, and he lost his focus. So if somebody says to you, "Hey, Bob, let's bag the sales meeting and instead attend fashion shows in Europe," just say no.
- Momentum is very important. Donald Trump personally knew the famous developer William Levitt, and he lost *his* momentum, and it sucked.

- You need a good assistant. Donald Trump had an assistant once who was a real babe, but her English was poor, so she didn't recognize some of the famous people who called Donald Trump, including, quote, "the likes of Hugh Grant, Reggie Jackson, George Steinbrenner, Jack Welch, Paul Anka, Mohamed Al Fayed, Regis Philbin, or Tony Bennett."
- That's right: Donald Trump personally knows *Paul Anka.*
- Work hard! Donald Trump works hard.
- Be blunt! Donald Trump is blunt.
- You need to hire good people. (Yes, Donald Trump already made this point earlier, but it is very important.)
- Some ideas are good, and some are not. Know the difference! Donald Trump does.
- As has been noted in earlier chapters, it's important to have good people around you. Donald Trump has a lot of terrific people around him, including one named Matthew Calamari, which I believe is Italian for "squid," although Mr. Trump does not state this in his book.
- Keep learning! Learning is good. Donald Trump and Aldous Huxley (a famous author) are two examples of big learners.
- Think big! Donald Trump thinks big.
- When you ask for a raise, do it at the right time, not at the wrong time.
- Play golf. It's terrific! Donald Trump plays golf and also owns several golf courses named after him. They're terrific courses.
- Don't be afraid to toot your own horn. By tooting *his* own horn, Donald Trump has turned the name "Trump" into a famous brand name, like "Rolls-Royce." As Donald Trump states in *TRUMP: How to Get Rich:*

When I remember the line from Shakespeare's Romeo and Juliet—
*"What's in a name?"—I have to laugh. What's in a name can be
far more than either the Bard or I ever could have imagined.*[42]

- When you're a huge success like Donald Trump, critics will take shots at you. Donald Trump doesn't care!

- Trust your gut instincts. Donald Trump does. This is based on the work of Carl Jung, a famous person Donald Trump is familiar with, like Shakespeare and Paul Anka.

- In 2000, Donald Trump considered running for president, and he had some terrific ideas, but then he decided not to, because he would have been a pathetic joke.

- No! Just kidding! He decided not to because he is too darned blunt for politics.

- You shouldn't shake hands. Hands have germs on them, and sometimes pee. Yuck! Donald Trump has given this a *lot* of thought.

- One time Anthony Robbins, the motivational guy with teeth the size of storm shutters, paid Donald Trump, quote, "a great deal of money" to give a speech in front of twenty thousand people. A lot of people would have been nervous. Not Donald Trump! The speech was terrific.

- Tony Robbins is a terrific guy. Donald Trump wholeheartedly endorses him.

- When you give a speech, you should be entertaining. Examples of great entertainers are Elvis Presley, Wayne Newton, Liberace, Frank Sinatra, and Regis Philbin. "Study Regis Philbin," Donald Trump advises.

---

42. Although some scholars believe that when the Bard wrote this particular line, he might not have been referring to branding.

- You need a good attitude. Here's a direct quote from Donald Trump about attitude: "What's the altitude of your attitude? Is it a high frequency or low frequency? Having a high frequency will attune you to a wavelength that exudes confidence and clear-sighted enthusiasm."[43]
- Abraham Lincoln had a good attitude.
- You should read Carl Jung and have insights into yourself. Donald Trump does this.
- Donald Trump also reads Socrates and agrees with him.
- Make *sure* you have a prenuptial agreement. Donald Trump did, and boy was he glad.
- Thoreau would have had a prenuptial agreement.[44]
- Take control of your finances! Wayne Newton[45] is a personal friend of Donald Trump's. He was in a financial mess and asked Donald Trump what to do. Donald Trump told him: Take control of your finances! Wayne did, and it worked out. This lesson applies to everybody, not just famous celebrities.
- Donald Trump doesn't like doctors. "I think that, generally, they are a bunch of money-grubbing dogs," he states. He knows of a LOT of doctors who are bad. "I just can't stand the bastards," he notes.
- Be a good negotiator. Donald Trump is a terrific negotiator.
- Mario Cuomo is a shmuck. So is another man named Pete Dawkins.
- Donald Trump *likes* his hairstyle. "Personally, I think it looks good," he states.

---

43. I have no idea what this means, either.
44. Donald Trump actually appears to be asserting this about Thoreau.
45. A terrific entertainer.

- It's his natural hair, although he does color it.[46]
- A woman named Joy Behar has repeatedly attacked Donald Trump's hair, and he doesn't like her one bit. He states that she has "no talent and a terrible accent."
- Donald Trump is very rich, but he also has a terrific family and a lot of terrific friends, most of whom are also very rich.
- His wife, Melania Knauss, is a total babe, but also "a very calm and soothing person."
- Tom Brady is a terrific quarterback.
- Donald Trump is extremely busy. To illustrate this, from page 166 to page 209 he lists his schedule for an entire week, meeting by meeting and phone call by phone call. Here are a few excerpts: "I look over some kitchen and bathroom fixtures, and we decide to go with the top of the line. . . . Norma comes in to tell me that Oscar de la Renta is on the line. . . . I return Regis Philbin's call. . . . I take a call from Hugh Grant. . . . I return a few calls, including one to Larry King, one of the sharpest interviewers of all time. . . . This morning I have an interview with the legendary Barbara Walters.[47] . . . Sandra Bullock is here to visit. . . . Reggie Jackson stops by for a quick visit. . . . I go golfing with Carl Jung.[48] . . ."
- *The Apprentice,* which is the hit reality TV show that Donald Trump stars in, is a terrific show, with a lot of terrific people.
- Donald Trump owns a lot of big properties, which are listed on pages 231 to 244.
- On pages 245 to 248 are pictures of people in the Trump organization. They look like good people.

---

46. No shit.
47. A legend.
48. This last one is a joke. But only barely.

- The book was set in Galliard, a typeface designed by Matthew Carter for the Mergenthaler Linotype Company in 1978. It's based on the sixteenth-century typefaces of Robert Granjon.

So there you have it, in summary form: The Donald Trump system for getting rich. It's a terrific system, with a lot of practical applications in everyday life. Like, if somebody says to you, "Do you think we should go with the good idea? Or the bad idea?" You'd think to yourself: "What would Donald Trump do?" And immediately the answer would come to you: *He would take a call from Regis Philbin.*

Of course, it's not fair that you should get the benefits of Donald Trump's valuable thinking without paying for it. So you'll want to be sure to get his book. It retails for $21.95, and it's in bookstores everywhere. Go buy it right now![49]

49.

19

A GUIDE TO TIPPING

Just Do It

WHY DO WE TIP?
The main reason, of course, is that we have a simple, generous desire to express, in tangible form, our hope that our server did not spit in our entrée. But we also tip for other special services. Let me illustrate with a true story:

Some years ago I was on a book tour, which is when you go all around the country promoting a book, kind of like a prostitute, only with less dignity. You will never see a prostitute drum up business by going on a radio show and making armpit farts into a microphone. I have done this to promote a book.

Anyway, I was in Los Angeles, and the publisher put me up at a very swank hotel, the kind of hotel where everybody who works there, including rodents, is wearing a tuxedo. When I arrived, a bellperson instantly materialized and grabbed my luggage, which consisted of a small carry-on bag about the weight of a standard bagel. The bellperson carried this for me to the reception desk, a distance of, I would estimate, nineteen feet. It goes without saying that I had to tip him for rendering this service, so I pulled out a dollar and handed it to him, at which point he dematerialized.

I then checked in, and when I was finished, the reception-desk person made a gesture, and a second bellperson picked up my bagel and led me to my room, where he briefed me on the various hotel room features, such as, if I wanted the room to be warmer or cooler, I should adjust the thermostat accordingly; and that if I wanted to watch the television, I should turn it on. That kind of information does not come cheap, so I tipped him five dollars.

Now I was in the room, and I thought I was safe from having any more services rendered on me. But moments later there was a knock at the door; it was a tuxedo-wearing person, bringing me ice. I don't know why; I had not asked for ice. Perhaps the hotel staff had heard me on the radio and thought I would need to cool down my armpit. But, for whatever reason, there was the ice, in a very nice silver bucket, and I felt compelled to show my appreciation by giving the employee my only remaining smallish bill, which was a five.

Moments later, the doorbell rang *again*. I was hoping it was the ice guy, realizing he made a mistake, coming back to retrieve the ice and give me back my five. But no, it was *another* tuxedoed hotel employee, and she was bringing what she called an "amenity," which turned out to be: strawberries. As it happens, I hate strawberries. I would rather chew on a rat testicle than eat a strawberry. But this person had brought me a whole tastefully arranged tray of strawberries, enough strawberries to feed five people who actually liked them, and I had to give her *something,* and unfortunately the smallest bill I had left was a twenty. She didn't seem surprised to get such a generous tip; I imagine it's well known in the swank-hotel-employee world that the strawberry-bringer has a better chance of getting the higher-denomination bills, since the lower ones have already been collected by the ice-bringer and the two bagel-toters.

So at this point, having been at the hotel for maybe fifteen minutes, I was out $31 in tips. Granted, I had plenty of both ice and strawberries, but I was running low on cash. So for the rest of the evening I huddled in my room and refused to open the door, because there was no telling—once the word got around that I was out of small bills—what they would bring to me next. ("Mr. Barry, I brought you a croquet set. And Raoul is here with your pony.")

The point is that you need to carry plenty of cash if you expect to find yourself in certain tip-intensive situations, such as a nice hotel, a good restaurant, anywhere within a 200-mile radius of New York City, or an IRS audit. Also you must learn to give the tip in a suave manner. Do not wave the bill around like a battle flag and say: "Here! I am giving you some money as a tip!" You should slip the tip to the person via a subtle move, disguising the act as a simple handshake. Note how the sophisticated individuals shown in the following photographs are doing it. You can barely tell that money is changing hands:

Tipping in Restaurants

The most common tipping situation is restaurants, where servers often make a very low guaranteed wage and depend on tips for much, sometimes most, of their income. The basic formula in the United States is that, if the service is decent, you tip a minimum of 15 percent of the total bill. This is a simple concept, although some people seem to be unable to grasp it. These people are called "Canadians."

No, I am just poking a little good-natured fun at our friendly neighbors to the north. It is wrong to brand ALL Canadians as bad tippers, just because 99.9997 percent of them are.

But seriously, the sad truth is that there are many people, even non-Canadians, who seem to be simply unable to grasp the concept of tipping the server. We have all known such people. We have all gone to meals with them. They're the ones who, when the bill comes, figure out *exactly* how much they owe, to the penny, and put this amount into the communal pot, as if they expect the Tip Fairy to come flitting down out of the sky and add something for the server.

Sometimes these people don't put in enough even to cover their share of the bill. In my early days in the newspaper business, I used to go to lunch with a group of young reporters that included a guy named Art, who never came *close* to putting in enough money. Art had some specific amount in his head, like $2.35, that he believed all his meals were supposed to cost. No matter where we ate, and no matter what we ordered, when the bill came, Art would put in his $2.35. Sometimes somebody would call him on this, pointing out, "Art, there are six of us, and the bill is $87.50, and you had two cheeseburgers, an order of onion rings, and six beers." And so Art, very reluctantly, like a man parting with his lone remaining kidney, would grudgingly toss in another quarter.

You don't want to be like that, because it's unfair to the server and to your friends, and years later one of them could write a book and ridicule you using your real name. No, you always want to pay your fair share of the bill, and you want to add at least a 15 percent tip for decent service.

Of course you should knock the tip down if the server is rude, or inattentive, or overwhelmingly French. On the other hand, you should *increase* the tip if the service is good. You should also increase it if you are an annoying diner. The problem is that, if you are a truly annoying diner, you probably don't *know* you're annoying. So to help you out, I have prepared the following table, which will help you determine how annoying you are, and how much you need to add to the tip to compensate for this:

Tip Calculation Table for Annoying Diners

Annoying Behavior on Your Part	How Much You Should Increase Your Tip
You summon the server by snapping your fingers.	Add 2 percent per snap.
After poring over the menu for twenty minutes, you summon the server and announce that you are ready to place your order. Then, while the server is standing there, order pad in hand, you proceed to slooowly go through the entire menu, discussing the pros and cons of each item with your fellow diners and ignoring the server. You ultimately take longer to order your food than Franklin D. Roosevelt took to ask Congress for a declaration of war against Japan.	Add 3 percent for each minute that it takes you to order. Double this amount if you later change your order.
You never want your entrée prepared the way the restaurant usually prepares it. You say things like, "I'll have the baked filet of sole with spinach-cheese stuffing and lobster sauce, but instead of sole I want perch, and I want it pan-fried instead of baked, and instead of spinach and cheese I want a rutabaga chutney, and instead of lobster I want free-range mussels, and instead of a circular plate I want . . ."	Add 5 percent. Also consider just staying home and cooking your own meal.

Annoying Behavior on Your Part	How Much You Should Increase Your Tip
You ask the server to bring everything "on the side." You want the salad dressing separate from the salad, the lemon separate from the iced tea, the spaghetti sauce separate from the spaghetti, and the ice separate from the ice water, in which you want the hydrogen molecules separate from the oxygen molecules.	Add 2 percent for each thing on the side. Add another 5 percent if, when you get a thing on the side, you dump all of it into the thing it was on the side of, thereby nullifying whatever purpose was served by getting it on the side in the first place.
You call the server, who is a grown man or woman, "Hon."	Add a flat five dollars per "Hon."
You never allow the server to come within fifteen feet of your table without summoning him or her and sending him or her off on an errand to bring you something. You need many, many things, but you always ask for them *one thing at a time*. You never say, "I need Tabasco sauce and another spoon." Instead, you send the server for Tabasco sauce, and, when he or she returns, *then* you ask for the spoon. It apparently does not occur to you that the server may have other people to wait on. As far as you're concerned, the server is there solely to participate in your little Scavenger Hunt from Hell.	Add 10 percent.
No matter what you ordered, you *always* find something wrong with your entrée, and you *always* send it back to be cooked more, or cooked less, or be blessed by a priest, or something. You can *never* just eat your freaking food.	Add 10 percent.
In the end, no matter what kind of restaurant it is, and no matter how much everybody else enjoyed the meal, you are always dissatisfied. You often say, "I'm never going to eat there again!" One by one, you are ruling out every restaurant on the planet for being beneath your standards.	Never mind the tip. Please just eat somewhere else. Thank you.

Note that if you do *all* of the annoying things listed in this table, you could wind up being obligated to leave a tip that is close to 100 percent of your bill. But trust me: If you do all of these things, you're worth it.

TIPPING AT RESTAURANTS AND CAFÉS IN EUROPE

For Americans, tipping at a restaurant or café in Europe is scary. For one thing, the unit of currency used in most of Europe now is the "euro," and there is no way to know, without being Stephen Hawking, how much a euro is. The exchange rate is always some number that looks vaguely like pi, such as 1.85732. On top of that, the European tipping system is extremely confusing for Americans.

First off, the Europeans themselves do not tip. They don't have to tip, because they *never actually leave the restaurant or café.* They will sit there for days, weeks, *months,* drinking a single cup of coffee. They can do this because they have much more humanistic employment rules over there, where you only have to work thirty-five hours per year, and you get forty-seven weeks paid vacation, plus if you have a baby, or your domestic partner has a baby, or you were at one time yourself a baby, you get like sixteen years of paid leave. So there is really no compelling reason for a European person ever to leave a restaurant or café, which renders the tip issue pretty much moot.

For Americans it is different. Americans are over there on their two-week annual vacation, so their time is limited. They need to eat and leave, so they can resume the job of trudging around looking at cathedrals and trying to figure out what the hell a "flying buttress" is, and why anybody cares. This means that at some point, American tourists will need to pay the bill. They will wave to the waiter and pretend to scribble on their hands, which is the international hand gesture for "I am pretending to scribble on my hand." The waiter will then write something on a piece of paper and hand it to them. It will look like this:

The Americans will study this for a while, trying to figure out whether it is a number, and if so *what* number, and, above all, whether it includes a tip. They may even attempt to ask the waiter about this; if so, he will respond with a shrug that could mean "Yes," or "No," or "Just pay the stupid bill, because in twenty minutes I get off work for the rest of the year."

Sometimes the Americans will consult a guidebook, which will helpfully inform them that *usually* a service charge is included, but not *always,* and *sometimes* it is appropriate to add more, although the guidebook does not say *when,* or how *much* more. The Americans will spend twenty minutes or so trying to mentally divide or multiply—they are not sure which—by 1.85732. Finally, they will put down an amount of euros roughly equivalent to the annual budget of Liechtenstein. Then they will nervously slink away from the café to resume looking at buttresses, leaving the other café patrons to shake their heads, sip their coffees, and wonder how the hell a nation as clueless as America ever became a major world power.

Tipping Taxi Drivers in Foreign Countries

You should tip taxi drivers 10 percent, and increase this to 20 percent if they perform some special service, such as getting you to your destination alive.

Tipping Bathroom Attendants in Foreign Countries

You should not go to the bathroom in foreign countries.

20

SAVING MONEY ON TRAVEL

Good Luck

TRAVEL IS AN EXCELLENT WAY to escape from your boring, everyday lifestyle and visit places where you cannot easily locate the restrooms. Also, if you go abroad, travel gives you an opportunity to be exposed to other cultures and learn interesting things about them, such as: Do they speak English? Do they have any American food? Do they at least have ketchup?

Of course, travel is not free. In addition to the basic expenses of transportation, food, and lodging, you also need to budget incidentals such as T-shirts, souvenirs, bribes, antibiotics, surgery, and ransom. So, rule number one of travel is: *Take money.*

One way to take money is in the form of traveler's checks. The way these work is, you give a traveler's check company a bunch of money, and the traveler's check company gives you some checks. You cash some of these checks on your trip, and when you get home you put the rest of them in the back of your sock drawer for safekeeping, and then you forget all about them. Eventually you die, and the traveler's check company gets to keep the money you paid for the uncashed checks forever.

So traveler's checks are very popular with traveler's check companies. But they are not always such a big hit with regular humans such as cashiers and waiters, who, when you ask them if they take traveler's checks, will sometimes roll their eyes and demand photo ID and generally act as though you are trying to pay them with grocery coupons. Also, in many countries traveler's checks are not accepted as ransom.

The one big advantage of traveler's checks, of course, is that if you lose them, the traveler's check company will replace them promptly and without hassle. We know this because, in the TV commercials for traveler's checks, the person who loses the checks always gets replacement checks within seconds, and thus is able to resume enjoying his or her carefree vacation on the Planet Haboonda.

Here on the planet Earth, however, replacing lost or stolen traveler's checks is not always quite so simple. I base this statement on an experience I had several years ago involving my son, who, in the interest of protecting his identity, I will refer to here as "Fobert." When Fobert was nineteen, he went to Europe on a backpacking trip. I bought him some traveler's checks from a company that, in the interest of protecting its identity, I will refer to here as "Fisa." I figured this was a safe choice, since Fisa is a large company with many high-quality commercials, and their official Fisa Internet site stated that you could, quote, "easily get a refund if your cheques are lost or stolen."

Anyway, to make a long—you have *no idea*—story short, Fobert's traveler's checks were lost or stolen. His passport was also gone. This somehow happened when he was *on the plane going to*

Europe, which I believe is an international-traveler record for losing all your really important possessions.

So Fobert arrived in Europe with no money, and no proof of
citizenship. Fortunately he landed in a nation that, in the interest
of protecting its identity, I will refer to as Fermany—a casual, laid-
back, no-rules kind of place whose Official National Motto is,
"Whatever."

But seriously, the Fermans were pretty good sports about it,
holding Fobert for a mere eight hours and never once bringing
out the cattle prod. When Fobert finally got out of custody, the
U.S. consulate quickly gave him a new passport. And getting the
traveler's checks replaced turned out to be every bit as easy as
the Fisa company had promised, provided that you define "easy"
as "extremely hard."

Over the next two weeks, I made numerous telephone calls to
a Fisa office in Europe, which in case you were wondering is not a
local call from my house. The Fisa people kept telling me they
were investigating the matter, but for days they would not tell me
what they were investigating, nor when they expected to be finished. Finally, one of them revealed to me that they were trying to
determine whether Fobert had been "careless." This caused me
to momentarily lose my temper and shout, "OF *COURSE* HE
WAS CARELESS! HE'S A TEENAGE BOY AND HE'S CARE-
LESS AND HE LOSES THINGS! THAT'S WHY I BOUGHT
HIM YOUR [*very bad word that, in the interest of protecting its identity,
I will refer to as "wucking"*] TRAVELER'S CHECKS!"

Finally, after many testy phone calls from me, the Fisa people refunded the money. By then, Fobert was back in the United States, having completed his trip with money I sent to him via Festern Funion.

What is the moral here? The moral is that traveler's checks, at least Fisa traveler's checks, are a wonderful idea, provided that you are not careless. In other words, you should buy them only if you will never actually need them. The other moral is that if you permit your teenage child to travel alone to Europe, you are out of your wucking mind.

Another option is to use credit cards, which are lightweight and widely accepted, plus there is always the hope that your plane will crash on the way home and you won't have to pay the credit card company back. The disadvantage of credit cards is that, if you use them in foreign countries that use foreign currencies such as the peso or the kilometer, you will have no idea what you are actually paying for anything, which means that when you get home and open up your credit card bill, you could discover that when you were in Cairo, you paid $16,000 for a Snickers.

This is why, when I travel, I always carry cash. The danger with cash, of course, is that it makes you a target for professional pickpockets, who, especially in foreign tourist destinations, are so skillful that you won't notice them until your money is gone. In the photographs below, see if you can spot the professional pickpocket. He's in all four of the photos, but he's hard to find because he has mastered the art of using costumes and disguises to blend into any environment:

Which One Is the Pickpocket?

SOURCE: Scotland Yard

See? You can pore over these photos for hours without spotting the pickpocket! That's how clever these people are. And that's why, when you travel abroad with cash, you should do what seasoned world travelers have been doing for years: *Keep your money securely in your underpants.* This is usually the last place that a pickpocket thinks to look. Another advantage is, when you get a bill at a restaurant, and you start fishing around inside your drawers for the cash, sometimes the waiter will let you have the meal for free.

Speaking of being unwanted, another important security tip for foreign travel is: *Do not look like an American.* As a nation, we

Americans have spent many decades, and trillions of dollars, trying our best to make the rest of the world want to be friends with us, and as a result the rest of the world hates us. This is especially true in places such as Europe, Asia, Africa, South America, Central America, Antarctica, the Moon, and pockets of North America, including Mexico, Canada, and Manhattan Island.

If you plan to travel to any of these areas, for your own safety you must create the impression that you're not from the United States. Rule one is: *Do not wear sneakers.* I don't know why, but the first thing most Americans do, when they're getting ready for a trip, is go to the mall and purchase new, blindingly white sneakers. Your chunkier, more sedentary Americans also choose to travel in athletic-style warm-up suits, as though they expect to be competing in the 200-meter hurdles, when in fact they will not be doing anything more active on their trip than pointing at the dessert cart.

The result is that a foreign pickpocket can easily spot American tourists: They're the ones who look like the Senior Weight Watchers track team. You do *not* want this look. You should dress to blend into the local environment, as we see in these examples:

How to Dress So Foreigners Won't Know You're American

Wrong   **Right**   **Wrong**   **Right**

Another good way to blend in when you travel abroad is to speak a foreign language. Most Americans cannot do this, because they speak only English. When confronted with a foreign person who does not speak English, Americans will generally seek to bridge the language gap by speaking English louder ("IS THERE A BIGGER *MONA LISA* AROUND ANYWHERE?"). So if you want to appear non-American, it helps if you know at least a smattering of some foreign language. Here's a list of useful phrases you can memorize:

Useful French Phrases

- Où est l'Internet? *(Where is the Internet?)*
- Comment venir ces portions sont si sacrées petites? *(How come these portions are so darned small?)*
- Nous voulons un REPAS, zut, pas un d'oeuvre de hors piquere une crise. *(We want a MEAL, dammit, not a freaking hors d'oeuvre.)*
- Ces Américains! Qu'un paquet d'idiots! Nous nous sont de la Scandinavie. *(Those Americans! What a bunch of idiots! We ourselves are from Scandinavia.)*

Useful Italian Phrases

- Dov'è il Internet? *(Where is the Internet?)*
- Ci sono qualunque gabinetti PULITI in questo paese? *(Are there any CLEAN toilets in this country?)*
- Quanto costa vedere il Papa? *(How much does it cost to see the Pope?)*
- Lei tenta di dirme che siamo venuti tutta la maniera da New Jersey—l'attesa no, io Scandinavia media—soltanto di scoprire che IL PAPA NON È DISPONIBILE? *(Are you trying*

*to tell me that we came all the way from New Jersey—no, wait,
I mean Scandinavia—only to find out that THE POPE IS NOT
AVAILABLE?)*

USEFUL GERMAN PHRASES

- Wo ist das Internet? *(Where is the Internet?)*
- Junge, Sie können Leute keinen Weltkrieg, NICHT wahr,
  gewinnen? *(Boy, you people CANNOT win a world war, can you?)*
- Die Amerikaner haben wirklich Ihre Esel, nicht wahr ge-
  treten? Nicht, dass es irgendein großes Geschäft zu uns Skan-
  dinavier ist. *(The Americans really kicked your asses, didn't they?
  Not that it's any big deal to us Scandinavians.)*
- Ich werde Sie dies geben: Sie haben ausgezeichnete Toilet-
  ten. *(I'll give you this: You have excellent toilets.)*

USEFUL SPANISH PHRASES

- ¿Dónde está el Internet? *(Where is the Internet?)*
- ¿Esta España es, o México? Yo nunca los puedo decir aparte.
  (Is this Spain or Mexico? I can never tell them apart.)
- Sé uno de ellos le da diarrea. *(I know one of them gives you
  diarrhea.)*
- Nosotros no tenemos tequila en nuestra nación de hogar de
  Scandinavia. *(We do not have tequila in our home nation of Scan-
  dinavia.)*
- ¡Oye! ¡Hay un abigarrando GUSANO en esta botella! *(Hey!
  There is a freaking WORM in this bottle!)*
- Usted mira un pleito grave, el señor. *(You are looking at a seri-
  ous lawsuit, mister.)*
- Yo no cuido si soy una tradición. Usted perderá sus calzoncil-

los. *(I don't care if it's a tradition. You are going to lose your under-shorts.)*

USEFUL JAPANESE PHRASES

- 男 麻 恵 *(Where is the Internet?)*
- 男 麻 恵 *(What the hell kind of food is this?)*
- 男 麻 恵 *(You mean people actually EAT this?)*
- 男 麻 恵 *(Do you have any entrées WITHOUT eyeballs?)*
- 男 麻 恵 *(How do you pronounce this Japanese writing?)*
- 男 麻 恵 *(Even in Scandinavia, which is where we come from, we are still a little ticked off about Pearl Harbor.)*

USEFUL CHINESE PHRASES

- て美しい *(Where is the Internet?)*
- 日本語文 *(We're not from around here. We're from Scandinavia, which is a completely different country from the United States.)*
- 凛として *(God, there's like MILLIONS of you people.)*
- 美しい日 *(Seriously, how do you tell yourselves apart?)*
- い日本語 *(I don't get what's so great about this wall.)*

Traveling by Air

Airplanes have really changed the way we travel. In the old days, it could take you literally days to get from New York to Chicago. Now you can simply board a plane at one of the New York metropolitan area's three convenient airports,[50] and in just a couple of

---

50. Kennedy, La Guardia, and Newark. Allow three hours to get to any of these airports, unless of course it is rush hour, in which case your best bet is to drive to the airport in Cleveland.

hours, you will be informed that there is a problem with the warning light on the auxiliary deframbulation extrapolator, and the replacement part has to be brought in from Pittsburgh via canoe, so your flight will not be taking off during the current lunar cycle.

Mechanical delays happen a lot, because airplanes are gigantic complicated machines containing literally millions of parts. Nobody really understands how they work. Every time a flight takes off, the airline mechanics exchange high fives to celebrate the fact that (a) the plane actually got off the ground, and (b) they are not on it. A major reason why the pilots keep the cockpit door shut during flights is so you can't see them thumbing through the airplane owner's manual, trying to figure out what the hell all those instruments and switches *do*.

In addition to mechanical problems, flights are often delayed by bad weather, as pilots often must divert the plane hundreds of miles from the planned route so that they can fly directly into violent storms and cause the plane to shake like a giant paint mixer. This is the only real fun pilots have. If they're in a frisky mood, they'll fly a plane through the same thundercloud four or five times.

But the point is that there's a lot of uncertainty connected with air travel, which is why the first rule for airline passengers is: *Be flexible.* Don't be hampered by rigid, preconceived notions of exactly when, or exactly where, the airplane is going to go. If you're planning to fly from Detroit to London on a certain day, be open to the possibility that you will not necessarily leave on that day, and that you might land in some city other than London, such as Milwaukee, which also offers plenty to see and do.

The second rule for airline passengers is: *Shop around for the lowest fare.* Buying an airline ticket is very similar to buying a lotto ticket, only with more of an element of chance. Most airlines offer many different fares for each flight, and the fares are constantly changing. Neither you, nor anybody else on the planet including Stephen Hawking, can know ahead of time what random fare the airline computer will decide to charge you.

Say you want to fly from Phoenix to Minneapolis. You go to an Internet travel site, and the computer gives you a roundtrip fare of $159. So you turn to your spouse and say, "Hey, Marge or Bob, depending on your gender! I got us a pretty good price to Minneapolis!"

But when you turn back to your computer screen, BAM, the airline fare computer—which can see you through your computer screen and loves to play pranks—suddenly increases your fare to $386. While you're absorbing this bad news, BAM, the fare suddenly drops to $17, provided you fly on a weekday containing three or more vowels. This looks like a good deal, so you try to click on it, but before you can, BAM, the fare changes to a flat $7,000 for nonrefundable coach. If you listen carefully, you can actually hear the airline computer chuckling at the expression on your face.

Sometimes an airline computer will get in a really silly mood and decide to change all the fares for a particular flight *while the plane is in the air*. This means the flight attendants have to pass through the cabin taking money away from some passengers and handing it over to others.

This constant changing of airline fares is very annoying to passengers, but there's a simple, sound reason why the airlines use this system: They want to annoy their passengers.

No, seriously, there really is a rational economic reason why airline fares are completely insane. I've had it explained to me several times, and although I don't totally understand it, it has something to do with supply and demand and load factors as they relate to the auxiliary deframbulation extrapolator. But never mind the reason. The point is that you can get lower fares if you're willing to shop around and check for special airline promotions and deals. For example, some airlines will offer discounts if you will agree to sit next to a screaming baby or a large flatulent man with Death Star BO. I get that particular deal all the time.

You also can often get a lower fare by taking connecting, instead of direct, flights. For example, in the case of the Phoenix-to-Minneapolis trip, you can save as much as 30 percent if you don't mind a two-day layover in Atlanta. Not only will you be paying less, but there's always a chance that your Phoenix-Atlanta flight will, for one wacky airline reason or another, wind up landing in Minneapolis anyway. Or even London! There's lots to see and do in London.

Here's some other helpful information on traveling by air:

Luggage

One option for your luggage is to check it in with the airline. This combines the convenience of not having to lug a bunch of possessions through the airport with the comfort of knowing that you may never see your possessions again. Astronomers using powerful telescopes have detected missing luggage in other galaxies.

The other option is to carry your luggage onto the plane. The key point to remember here is that your luggage must be able to fit into the overhead luggage bin. Let me repeat that:

YOUR CARRY-ON LUGGAGE MUST ACTUALLY FIT *INSIDE* THE LUGGAGE COMPARTMENT.

Or, to put it another way:

YOUR CARRY-ON LUGGAGE NEEDS TO BE
SMALLER THAN THE LUGGAGE COMPARTMENT,
SO THAT IT CAN FIT INSIDE.

I apologize for shouting in boldfaced capital letters, but this
concept seems to be very difficult for many airline passengers to
grasp. I am a frequent flyer, and it seems as if every time I get on a
plane, there are passengers ahead of me hauling a suitcase that is
clearly larger than the overhead storage bin. Sometimes it's larger
than my first apartment. It's the Shaquille O'Neal of suitcases.

When these passengers get to their seats, they grab the suitcase handle and, emitting a grunt like a mating boar, heave the
suitcase up to the bin, where *BONK!* it bounces right off, because
of course it is too large to fit. It is *much* too large to fit. Anybody
with a rudimentary grasp of spatial relationships, including a reasonably sharp gerbil, can see immediately that any effort to put
this particular object into this particular space is—like the marriage of Michael Jackson and Lisa Marie Presley—doomed to fail.

But that does not stop these determined, spatially impaired
passengers. They grunt again, heave again, and *BONK!* the
Shaquille suitcase again bounces back. Meanwhile, of course, the
boarding process has ground to a halt, because the suitcase
heavers are blocking the airplane aisle, the way a dead possum
blocks a drainpipe.

Finally a flight attendant[51] will work her way through the crowd
and patiently explain to the passengers that they have to check
their giant suitcase. If she didn't stop them, they would keep

---

51. I could never be a flight attendant; I would last maybe two flights before I
killed a passenger with my bare hands.

grunting, heaving, and bonking it until they weakened the structure of the plane and large chunks of fuselage started to fall off.

True Fact: I have seen passengers *argue* with the flight attendant that their giant suitcase, which clearly does not fit into the overhead, *should* fit into the overhead, because—and this is a direct quote—"it's a carry-on suitcase." What they mean by this, I believe, is that the suitcase has wheels. So, let us note the following fact for the record: *Just because something has wheels, that does not mean you can carry it onto the airplane.* The following objects all have wheels, but not all of them will fit into the overhead storage compartment:

Yes   **Maybe**   **No**   **No**   **No**

I apologize for going on at such great length about this, but as you may have gathered, this is a pet peeve of mine. I promise to drop it now and move on with our tips for airline travel.

Airline Security

Before the Age of Terrorism, airline security was pretty relaxed. You could arrive at the airport five minutes before your plane was supposed to take off and sprint straight to your gate. If the plane had already left the gate, you could run out onto the runway, waving your arms. If a uniformed security person blocked your path, you could simply shove him aside and shout, "GET OUT OF MY

WAY, YOU FOOL! I HAVE A *PLANE TO CATCH!*" You could carry a flamethrower onto the plane, as long as you were not actively using it to throw flame. Sometimes, if the pilot was in a good mood or badly hungover, he'd let passengers come up to the cockpit and fly the plane. ("Hi, everybody! My name is Harmon Sperkle. I'm a sales representative in the ceramic tile line, but for the next hour or so I'll be your pilot while the captain takes a little nap. Let's see what happens when I pull on this *WHOOOOOAAA. . . .*")

Alas, those carefree days are gone. Today, if you want to travel by air, you must go through a series of rigorous tests designed to guard against the danger—which is always lurking, whether we want to think about it or not—that you might actually make your flight. Here are the security basics you need to know:

1. You should arrive at the airport well in advance of your scheduled flight departure time. The Transportation Safety Administration recommends that, for an 8 a.m. flight, you get to the airport "while it is still under construction." If you are not reading this book at the airport, you are too late.

2. Once you arrive at the airport, you need to get into a line. It doesn't matter which line. Just get into one. This is the heart of the airport security system. The idea is that when the terrorists get to the airport, they'll see these big lines everywhere, and they'll say the hell with it and go into some other line of work, such as customer service. If, when you arrive at the airport, you don't see any lines, you should get together with other travelers and organize one.

3. Eventually, after you have spent enough time in lines, you'll reach the security checkpoint. This is the part that confuses many people, so let's break it down into a series of simple steps:

- Have your photo ID and boarding pass ready. You will have plenty of time to get these out, because the person in front of you—despite passing eight signs that say, in large letters, HAVE YOUR PHOTO ID AND BOARDING PASS READY— will *not* have his or her photo ID and boarding pass ready. This person will also be towing a "carry-on" suitcase the size of a U-Haul trailer.
- When it's your turn, show your photo ID and boarding pass to the security person, who will frown at it in a practiced manner without actually looking at it.
- Put your photo ID away, but keep your boarding pass out. With your spare hand, carry your belongings to the X-ray machine.

Note: *The X-ray machine is perfectly safe for photographic film. It will make YOU sterile, but your film will be fine.*

- Still holding your boarding pass, use your other hand to get a plastic bin. Place your laptop computer, cell phone, flame-thrower, dentures, hearing aid, prosthetic limb, and children under two in this bin. Also remove your jacket, belt, shoes, and—if the terrorism alert level is Code Magenta or higher— your underwire brassiere.
- Using one hand to hold your boarding pass and the other to hold up your pants and a third hand to shield your bosom, shuffle through the metal detector in the meek and submissive manner employed by Dorothy, the Scarecrow, the Tin Man, and the Cowardly Lion when approaching the Wizard of Oz.

Note: *The metal detector is perfectly safe for humans. The fact that it causes the kidneys of laboratory rats to explode like cheap party balloons is, according to a U.S. government study, "probably a coincidence."*

That's all there is to it! You are now free to get dressed—using the convenient filthy airport floor provided for this purpose—then proceed to your gate to board your flight. Bon voyage!

Note: *Your flight has a problem with the auxiliary deframbulation extrapolator.*

But getting back to the topic of this book, which is money, here are some other tips for traveling on a budget:

Saving Money on Hotels

The key is toilet paper. You want to stay at a hotel where the toilet paper in your room looks like this:

You do *not* want to stay in a hotel where the end of the toilet-paper roll has been folded into a triangle, or—even worse—folded and then sealed, like this:

This means that the hotel is charging you at least $75 more per night than a comparable hotel with unfolded toilet paper.

The hotel industry has learned that when hotel guests see triangulated toilet paper, they think: "Wow! That is a classy touch!" As opposed to: "Yuck! They expect me to wipe my butt with somebody's origami project!"

So before checking into a hotel, always do what savvy travelers such as Regis Philbin and Barbara Walters do: *Ask at the front desk to see a sample roll of hotel toilet paper.* If it's folded, inform the hotel staff that you will be doing your business elsewhere.

Saving Money on Family Vacations

The best way to save money on a family vacation, according to the American Association of Travel Planning Professionals, is to "not take any members of your family."

21

PLANNING FOR YOUR
RETIREMENT

The Financial Advantages of Early Death

W E ALL DREAM OF RETIRING—of waking up each day knowing that we have no job to go to and are free to spend the day taking a walk, reading a book, or simply "kicking back" and relaxing in our appliance carton of a residence.

Because the truth is that most of us, if we stop working, will instantly become starving homeless persons. Why? Let's take a look at some sobering statistics:

- Every year, 200 Americans are killed by their own dental floss.
- In her brief nine-month lifetime, a single female cockroach can produce 16,000 young.

And the statistics for retirement are even more sobering. Many people today simply cannot afford to retire. The singing artist Cher, for example, was forced to keep her Farewell Tour going until she was routinely ejecting her dentures onstage. Another sad example is Queen Elizabeth II, who, faced with the high cost of castle upkeep and horse maintenance, had to keep on queening until her hands were shaking so badly that candidates for knighthood refused the honor for fear that they would be decapitated during the sword ceremony. Strom Thurmond of South Carolina was unable to retire from the U.S. Senate until he had been legally dead for six years.

This is the bleak future that you face if you fail to plan for your retirement. The time to do this is *right now*, so let's get started.

Step one is to create a detailed balance sheet showing your current financial situation in terms of assets and liabilities. This is really boring, so I've taken the trouble of doing it for you:

YOUR FINANCIAL BALANCE SHEET

Your Assets

Cash on hand in the form of spendable currency	$78.63
Cash on hand in the form of pennies that you will never get around to converting into actual money	$292.11
Cash under your car seat bonded by hardened ketchup to French fries dating back to 2001	$6.90
Checking account balance	$782.06
Checking account balance adjusted for outstanding checks	($1,803.69)
Savings account	0.00[52]
Stocks that you bought through your company's stock purchase plan, which seemed like a good investment until your company was managed into bankruptcy by an incompetent and possibly criminal CEO who would ultimately be punished by receiving a lavish golden-parachute settlement including at least two jets	$2,038.52[53]

---

52. You don't have a savings account, remember? You *meant* to open one, but you never got around to it because of all your other urgent financial priorities, such as his 'n' hers Jet Skis.

Cash value of life insurance	$0.00[54]
Equity in your home	$18,000.00
Equity in your home adjusted for the home equity loan you took out for an extensive and much-needed home-renovation project, although you wound up going to Vegas and investing the bulk of it in video poker	($12,000.00)
Estimated resale value of your cars, TVs, stereo, furniture, clothes, Jet Skis, and other possessions	$25,000.00
What you would actually get for your cars, TVs, stereo, furniture, clothes, Jet Skis, and other possessions if you somehow managed to sell them	$1,832.40

Your Liabilities

Credit card debt as of 8:30 this morning	$12,657.25[55]
Mortgage	$117,392.90[56]
Unpaid balance of loans you took out to send your children to colleges where they either dropped out after seven semesters to pursue careers in the field of street mime or, worse, majored in English	$53,4822.06
Bills owed	$3,985.63
More bills owed	$6,938.96
Still more freaking bills owed	$8,409.78
Liabilities that you don't realize you have, but, trust me, you do	$21,847.69

SOURCE: The Internet

---

53. This figure will drop to approximately zero later this week when SEC auditors announce that the corporate books reflect reality to about the same extent as *Horton Hears a Who*.

54. See "savings account."

55. At 27.5 percent interest, compounded hourly, this balance will be an even fifteen grand by noon.

56. This is a "fixed balance" type of mortgage, meaning no matter how many payments you make, you will still owe the bank $117,392.90 (see chapter titled "How to Get Rich in Real Estate").

Now, to see how much money you have available for your retirement, all we need to do is add up your assets and subtract your liabilities, which gives us a net total of . . .

. . . OK, without being too brutally specific, let's just say that, if you're relying on your current assets, it does not look good for you to retire any time in the immediate millennium.

This means you need some way to continue getting money *after* you stop working. One source of money, of course, is your company pension, which will pay you a certain amount per month until such time as either (a) you die, or (b) your company goes out of business or is purchased by a vicious bloodsucking predator company, which, the way things are going, could happen later today.

Your other source for retirement income is Social Security, a federal program started by President Franklin D. "Teddy" Roosevelt during the Great Depression, which was caused when the Stock Market collapsed onto Wall Street, creating a huge Dust Bowl that crippled the U.S. economy, put millions out of work, ravaged countless lives, and forced many young men to wear knickers. It was a grim time, a time that older people still talk about today, causing younger people to creep quietly out of the room.

Out of this national trauma came our Social Security system. Here's how it works: Each pay period, your employer deducts a chunk of the money you have earned and sends it to the federal government, which holds it for safekeeping in a big sturdy vault surrounded by army tanks. When you retire, your money is waiting for you, along with your invisibility cloak and your magic time-travel ring.

Ha ha! As you may have gathered, I'm kidding 🖼. Your money is *not* waiting for you. Because the way Social Security *really* works is, the instant the federal government gets your money, it does the thing that governments do better than anybody else when it comes to money, which is spend it. Specifically, the government sends your former money to some elderly person, who uses it to buy food and shelter, unless this elderly person happens to be, say, Warren Buffet, in which case he uses it to tip the guy who washes his various helicopters.

But in any event, by the time you're ready to collect Social Security, all the money you paid in to the system will be long gone. This means that your Social Security money will have to come from the younger generation. There are two big problems with this:

Social Security Problem No. 1: *The younger generation is, with all due respect, worthless.*

This is a generation that doesn't even know which part of a baseball cap is supposed to go in front.[57] And do *not* get me started on music, OK? Do *not* make me remind you that this is the generation that gave us "hip-hop," a genre that requires essentially the same degree of musical skill as burping, as well as concert acts such as Britney Spears, whose "concert" consists of cavorting violently around the stage wearing pants cut so impossibly low in front that you begin to wonder whether Britney is in fact an anatomically correct human being, or if she had some of her key organs relocated to another part of her body, or perhaps her agent's body. But the point is that with all the audiovisual distractions at a modern $75-a-ticket stadium concert—the choreography, costumes, acrobats, giant TV screens, fireworks, jet flyovers, onstage boa constrictors, etc.—the one thing you are *not* particularly noticing is

---

57. Answer: the front part.

the music, which is just as well, because neither Britney nor any of the other people on the stage is actually singing anything—they're far too busy cavorting—which means the actual *music* is being produced somewhere backstage by a digital device about the size of a tin of Altoids. This device is the heart of the modern concert industry: It has its own bodyguards, personal trainer, manager, groupies,[58] etc., because without it, the show cannot go on, as was harshly demonstrated during a sold-out 1993 performance by the Backstreet Boys during which the Altoids tin was carried off by rats, shutting the music down entirely and forcing the artists to entertain the crowd with armpit farts.[59]

Oh, it was different in my day. In my day, the musicians made real music, and they made it *live.* Can you imagine Elvis Presley or Aretha Franklin prancing around and lip-synching? Of course not! You can't even imagine them prancing around without the aid of forklifts.

No sir, when I was young, if you went to a major rock concert, you knew what you were going to see on the stage: You were going to see a sweating promoter explaining why the act per se had not physically arrived yet. This happened a *lot* in the sixties. You'd be in a packed arena in, say, Philadelphia, to see a performance by The Who, and maybe two hours after the concert was scheduled to start, the promoter would appear onstage and say, "We have good news! The Who's plane has landed in New York! Once they clear Customs they'll be on their way!" Then, after some half-

---

58. In the form of scantily dressed pink iPods.
59. These were recorded and later released as the platinum-selling album *Odor of Love.*

hearted booing, the crowd would settle back in its seats and resume passing around doobies the size of yule logs. Sometimes The Who would, eventually, show up; sometimes The Who would not show up; sometimes there was frankly no way to tell. But whatever happened, it was *real,* and no matter how long it took, we audience members remained in our seats,[60] because we were committed to our music, not to mention incapable of movement.

That is the kind of dedication my generation is known for, and that, along with the threat of federal prison, is why we have always come through with our payments to the Social Security system, which as you may or may not recall is technically our topic.

Yes, we Baby Boomers paid for the retirement of the generation ahead of us. But will the younger generation do the same for us? Or will they at some point rise up in unison and say to us, quote: "Up yours, Baby Boomers! We're not paying for your retirement! We're sick of hearing you criticize us and our music! What about some of YOUR music? Do you have ANY IDEA how many wedding receptions and bar mitzvahs we've attended where we had to sit around watching you Boomers lurch around the floor doing some kind of spastic 1968 boogaloo to 'Jeremiah Was a Bullfrog,' thinking you were the coolest thing on two feet? Do you have ANY FREAKING IDEA how much we hate Jeremiah the freaking Bullfrog? And do you have any idea how tired we are of television commercials for products aimed at your various Boomer insecurities and ailments, such as the apparent inability—to judge from the number of ads for Viagra alone—of 93

---

60. Even as you read these words, somewhere in a hall in Philadelphia there is a guy wearing a tie-dyed T-shirt, still waiting for The Who.

percent of all American men over the age of forty-five to produce a workable erection? Has it occurred to you that the younger generation does not want to be constantly reminded about the limp, flaccid, shriveled state of its parents' sex life? Has it occurred to you that one possible reason why so many of you Boomer men can't get it up is that you keep watching these stupid ads *telling* you that you can't get it up?"

Oh yes, fellow Boomers, make no mistake: The younger generation loathes us and everything we stand[61] for. When the time comes for us to retire and start collecting Social Security, these young people are going to look for any petty excuse to avoid letting us have a chunk of their pay. One petty excuse they are likely to use is that, in a couple of decades, the chunk required to support us will be approximately 100 percent of their pay. This is because of the other problem with Social Security:

Social Security Problem No. 2:
There are too many Baby Boomers.

Another way of looking at this problem is that there are not enough members of the younger generation. We Boomers failed to produce a sufficient quantity of babies, and now, what with this nationwide erectile-dysfunction epidemic, it's too late.

And so when we analyze the financial future of the Social Security system, the numbers do not look good, as we see in this disturbing chart:

---

61. So to speak.

The Troubled Financial Future of Social Security

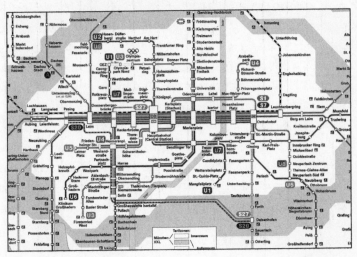

SOURCE: Visa

As this chart clearly shows, the Social Security system is headed for bankruptcy and total collapse unless it is reformed soon. The good news is, the leaders of both major political parties are well aware of this looming disaster and the need for prompt, decisive action. The bad news is, our political leaders could not take prompt, decisive action if their undershorts caught fire. The Democrats and Republicans have been debating what to do about Social Security for years now without producing anything other than accusations that their opponents are lying vermin scum. This is true as far as it goes, but it doesn't address the underlying problem.

So, to sum up your retirement situation:

1. You don't currently have enough money to retire.
2. You will probably *never* have enough money to retire.
3. Retirement-wise, you are up Shit Creek.

So maybe you should consider some alternatives to retiring, such as . . . OK, here's one: *not* retiring. Retirement is not necessarily a good thing, especially if you end up as an inmate in one of those "adult leisure communities" with a name like "Sunny Glades Glen III," the kind that always describe themselves with the words like "fun" and "active," as though they are one big wild happening party, when in fact many of the residents display no more vital signs than a frozen beef patty, and the "action" largely consists of elderly people driving golf carts to activities with names like "Low-Impact Senior-obics," wherein an enthusiastic instructor, accompanied by peppy music,[62] leads participants through a workout routine providing about the same degree of cardiovascular stimulation as operating a stapler.

So maybe retirement isn't so great. Maybe you'd be happier if you just kept working right on into old age. Of course, this might not be the best idea if you are, say, a brain surgeon:

YOU: OK, I'm ready to open the patient's skull. Nurse, hand me the saw.

NURSE: You're holding the saw.

YOU: I am? (*Looking down*) So I am! Ha ha! And is this the patient?

NURSE: No, that's your assistant, Dr. Whelkmonger.

YOU: Ah! So *this* must be the patient.

NURSE: No, that's an oxygen tank.

YOU (*examining tank*): Does it have medical insurance?

Maybe it's not such a great idea for you to continue working, either. But does that mean you have no options left for old age?

---

62. "Jeremiah Was a Bullfrog."

Heck no! There is no call for that kind of "negative Nelly" thinking! You still have time to salvage your retirement! All you need to do is develop some financial discipline, develop a realistic budget, avoid frivolous spending, pay off your debts, and start putting away a meaningful amount of money each month for the future. Don't be discouraged! You really *can* do it, if you put your mind to it and use your magic time-travel ring!

Note: You'll want to look for a refrigerator carton. Those are the roomiest.

22

PLANNING YOUR ESTATE

Urg

Y OU *ARE* GOING TO DIE. It's an unavoidable fact of nature that sooner or later, everybody passes away, except Keith Richards.[63] So your time will definitely come—probably not today, probably not tomorrow. But definitely sometime next week.

If you're like most people, though, you haven't given much thought to what will happen after you die, because at that point—so your reasoning goes—you'll be dead. You figure somebody else can deal with everything. This is also what keeps you from cleaning your garage.

This is a shortsighted and selfish attitude. There are some very important decisions that have to be made *before* you die, and *you* are the one who should make them.

The most important question, of course, is: What will your last words be? You should decide this in advance of kicking the actual bucket. If you wait until the last minute and have nothing prepared, you're going to end up uttering some lame, spur-of-the-moment last words, such as "Urg," or "Tell the nurse I have to

---

63. If Keith Richards is, in fact, dead when you read this, please substitute Cher.

make a number two." Is that what you want? Do you want your loved ones' final memory of you—your lifetime, your career, your accomplishments—to involve a bowel movement?

No, you want to leave them with some good, memorable last words, like the ones emitted by Civil War General John Sedgwick, who, moments before being fatally shot in the head in the battle of Spotsylvania, said: "They couldn't hit an elephant at this distance."[64] Granted, those are not *deep* last words, but they're *funny*. I bet everybody was cracking up at John's funeral.

If you don't want to go with funny, you can go with poignant. The last words of Louise, Queen of Prussia, in 1820 were: "I am a Queen, but I have not the power to move my arms." Of course you'd sound pretty stupid saying this if you were not, technically, a queen, but you could adapt it to your specific situation, as in: "I am the Cooterman Backhoe Rental Company's Assistant Regional Manager for Northern and Central Kentucky, but I have not the power to move my arms." A final quote like that is bound to produce feelings of admiration in your loved ones ("He must be on heavy drugs").

Another option is to go with prank last words. Your model here is the great American writer Henry David Thoreau, whose last words were—this is absolutely true—"Moose . . . Indian." Many people have tried to figure out what Henry meant by this, but it seems obvious to me: He was *messing* with people. Henry was a big kidder. So if you, like Henry, want to inject a note of fun into your final moments, consider saying dying words along these lines:

- •"My only dying request is that you all not make a big fuss over me after I'm gone. All I ask is that you think of me sometimes. Also I want to be buried next to Elvis."

---

64. **Really.**

- "I'm slipping away now. Everything is getting dark. Wait! I see a light ahead. . . . It's getting brighter. . . . It's . . . a Starbucks!"
- "Please send word of my death to my other spouse and children in New Zealand."
- "Before I go, there's something very important I must tell you all. *(Everybody leans closer.)* But first . . . Roo roo!"

Once you have your last words worked out, you need to give some thought to what you want done with your body after you die. May I make a suggestion here? Do NOT request to be cremated and have your ashes scattered at sea. This was a vaguely novel concept the first few hundred thousand times it was done, but these days *everybody* is being scattered at sea. Ships are running aground because of the dense fog of ashes swirling around the coastlines. The sea bottom is coated with a foot-thick layer of human sludge. Clams are dying needlessly by the millions.

The same goes for scattering ashes in a scenic land setting such as the Grand Canyon, which has been used so often for this purpose that it is now only about three feet deep. If you absolutely must have your ashes scattered, at least pick an original place, such as the "Small World" ride at Disney World, or a favorite salad bar.

An alternative to cremation is to have your body frozen, via a process called "cryogenics," from the ancient Greek words *cryogen,* meaning "to transform," and *ics,* meaning "into a human Dove Bar." The idea here is that at some point in the future, medical scientists, having run out of other things to do, will figure out a way to bring frozen dead people back to life. So you'll wake up in the year 2187[65] looking at some doctor who's not

---

65. Cher will still be on her Farewell Tour.

even born yet, who will hand you a bill for—allowing for inflation—seventy-three billion dollars, leaving you with no sound financial option but to kill yourself.

If you don't want to have anything funky done to your corpse, you can at least try to make your funeral entertaining. Remember: It's your funeral, so *they have to do what you tell them.* For example, you can leave explicit written instructions stating that, next to your casket, you want a tip jar. You can have the clergy member conducting the service say: "Let us pause for a moment of silence, during which we should try not to picture Camilla Parker-Bowles naked." Instead of some boring hymn, have the audience join together in singing the 1976 Captain & Tennille hit "Muskrat Love." Instead of a eulogy, have an Amway representative explain to your friends and loved ones the amazing power of multilevel marketing.

If you have any time left over after working out your last words, your body disposal, and your funeral, you might also want to take a few moments to figure out what will happen to your estate. Of course, if you follow the advice in this book, there's a strong chance you won't *have* an estate. But just in case, by some miracle, you're in danger of dying with a positive net worth, here's some information about estate planning, in the helpful "Q-and-A" format:

Q. What is estate planning?
A. Estate planning is when you plan your estate.
Q. Are the answers going to get any more helpful?
A. No.
Q. Why do I need estate planning?
A. If you don't have professional estate planning, a big chunk of your estate could be taken by taxes and lawyers.

Q. And professional estate planning will prevent that?

A. No, but it will guarantee that another chunk goes to professional estate planners.

Q. Do I need life insurance?

A. We put that question to the National Association of Life Insurance Salespersons Heavily Armed with Graphs.

Q. And what was their response?

A. They are surrounding your house right now.

Q. Do I need to make a will?

A. If you don't have a will, you will die intestate.

Q. Is that bad?

A. It is if you're a guy.

Q. Can I make my own will?

A. Yes, but you must use very specific legal wording, or it will have no more legal validity than a used Big Mac wrapper. Follow this format *exactly:*

LAST WILL AND TESTAMENT OF (*YOUR NAME*)

*I (*your name*), residing in (*your country*), (*your state*), (*your nine-digit zip code*), being of sound mind and having had no more than six beers so far today, do hereby at this juncture complete, finalize, conclude, and terminate the first sentence of this will. I further state, assert, affirm, declare, and just generally write down in writing that I hereby revoke, cancel, annul, rescind, retract, invalidate, and withdraw any previous will or codicil I may or may not have made, with the proviso and stipulation that I have no idea what a "codicil" is. I don't think I ever made one. Maybe that time in Tijuana.*

ARTICLE I
MARRIAGE AND CHILDREN

I am hereby legally owning up to one (1) spouse, (name of spouse), *and a brood of children with the following monikers:* (monikers of children). *God knows I did my best.*

ARTICLE II
THE QUARTERING OF SOLDIERS

No Soldier shall, in time of peace, be quartered in any house, without the consent of the Owner, nor in time of war, but in a manner to be prescribed by law.

ARTICLE III
THE DIVVYING UP OF THE ESTATE

I would like to bequeath $3.5 million in cash to be divided equally among my heirs. I would also like to shower naked with (name of hot movie star of the opposite gender such as Angelina Jolie). *But seriously, my heirs are welcome to go through my stuff and, if they find anything of value, divvy it up however they want, with the proviso and stipulation that, if they find any pornography, particularly the May 2002 issue of* Humongo Garbonzo *magazine under the NordicTrack machine in the basement, I don't know anything about that.*

ARTICLE IV
NOTE TO MY SPOUSE

Get rid of the damn NordicTrack. It was a mistake. I can admit this now that I'm dead. Also: It was me who peed in the laundry hamper at the Weeglemans' party.

ARTICLE V

SPECIAL NOTE TO MY CO-WORKER HARRY KRAMPNER,
WHO SAT IN THE CUBICLE NEXT TO MINE FOR EIGHT LONG YEARS

1. *Your views on U.S. immigration policy are ridiculous.*

2. *This is also true of your views on pretty much everything else you pontificated about when you were supposed to be working.*

3. *Basically, you are full of shit.*

4. *If you think nobody in the office notices what you do with your nose-pickings, think again.*

ARTICLE VI

A FINAL OBSERVATION

The quality of basketball free-throw shooting, at both the college and professional levels, has become a joke.

Signed,

(Your John Hancock)

John Hancock

Q. Are we still in the "Q-and-A" format?
A. Yes.

Q. What is a "Living Will"?
A. It is a document that tells doctors how hard you want them to try to keep you alive. Should they allow you to die, even if what you have is hemorrhoids? Or should they keep slapping electric paddles onto your chest and shouting "Clear!" long after insects have munched you down to a skeleton? Those are your two choices.

Q. Do you have any final words on estate planning?
A. Yes. They are "moose" and "Indian."

CONCLUSION: YOU *CAN* DO IT!

Maybe

N THE INTRODUCTION TO THIS BOOK, I promised that I would give you a set of proven, time-tested principles of money management. I believe that I have more than lived up to my end of the bargain, unless you count the part about giving you a set of proven, time-tested principles of money management.

But this book, as good as it is, can do only so much for you. At some point, you need to take matters into your own hands. You need to stop sitting on the sidelines, get into the game, pick up the ball, and run with it. Don't listen to the critics and the naysayers, who will try to discourage you with remarks like: "You'll never make it!" Or: "Put the ball down, you moron! We're playing billiards!"

Ignore these people. Don't give up! Remember that Bill Gates took nearly *six weeks* to make his first hundred million dollars. You must never doubt that you, like Bill, can achieve success. All you need to do is work hard, catch a few breaks, and know a bunch of information about computer software that is not included in this book.

I am not saying the road to financial success will always be smooth. You may stumble. You may fall. You may wind up in a hospital, where a psychopath posing as a nurse will inject you with a paralyzing drug and remove both of your eyeballs with a shrimp fork.

But you must not let these setbacks set you back. If, some day, you're feeling down, wondering if you're ever going to make it, remember the story of a young man by the name of Edison, who was trying to find a material that could be used as a filament in an electric lamp. He tried 2,000 different materials, and every one of them failed. Many people would have quit, but he did not. Late one night, he tried yet another material—the 2,001st—and you know what happened next: It also failed. So he bought a lottery ticket, and he won. (This was Thomas Edison's cousin, Steve Edison.)

There is no reason, other than the laws of probability, why the same thing cannot happen to you. But as you strive for financial success, remember this: Money is not everything. Oh, you may think it is. You may think, "If I had money, I would be happy." But remember: Money will not buy you true love. On the other hand, money will buy you a *lot* of high-quality fake love.

My point is that, given a choice between having money and not having money, you should definitely go with having it. And that, in the end, is why I wrote this book: to get your money.

No, seriously, I wrote this book to help you, and that is why I will end it with this promise, from me to you: If you follow the advice in this book, and you somehow fail to become wealthy, simply take this book back to the bookstore where you bought it, explain to the employees what happened, and ask for a full refund. You have my personal guarantee, right here in writing, that they will laugh until they blow snot into their lattes.

Until that time, I'd like to leave you with some words of wisdom. Unfortunately, at the moment, none come to mind. So instead I will leave you with this traditional Irish blessing:

> *May the road rise to meet you.*
> *May the wind be always at your back.*
> *May the sun shine warm upon your face,*
> *The rains fall soft upon your fields, and,*
> *Until we meet again,*
> *Moose. Indian.*

Photography Credits